M000205219

SQUIRTING MILK
AT CHAMELEONS
AN ACCIDENTAL AFRICAN

SIMON FENTON

Published in 2015
by Eye Books
29A Barrow Street
Much Wenlock
Shropshire
TF13 6EN
www.eye-books.com

ISBN: 978-1-903070-91-8

Copyright © Simon Fenton, 2015
Cover by Bert Stiekma and Simon Fenton

The moral right of the author has been asserted. All rights reserved.
No part of this publication may be reproduced, stored in a retrieval
system, or transmitted, in any form or by any means without
the prior written permission of the publisher, nor be otherwise
circulated in any form of binding or cover other than that in which
it is published and without a similar condition being imposed on
the subsequent purchaser.

British Library Cataloguing in Publication Data
A catalogue record for this book is available from the British Library

Printed by CPI Group (UK) Ltd, Croydon CR0 4YY

CONTENTS

To Khady, Gulliver and Alfie

SENEGAL AND THE CASAMANCE

MAURITANIA

MALI

GUINEA

THE GRIS-GRIS

The Baye Fall are Sufi mystics: a whirl of bright patchwork robes, beads and dreadlocks. In Dakar, one is trying to sell me some tourist tat, but he realises I don't have any money left. So we sit and chat around a fire on the sandy roadside. His name is Ibrahima and before long, he beats a rhythm with a plastic water bottle and chants:

"Simon, I wish you long life, I wish you good life ..."

Later, as I prepare to leave, Ibrahima pulls off one of his many necklaces, which consist of small leather pouches on cords.

"This a gris-gris, *wear it to protect you when you travel. Never take it off. Never give it to anyone."*

The day after I nearly died, I sat in the Senegalese gloom, sweating and aching, whilst a bare-chested black man vigorously rubbed my back. He took my head and violently cricked my neck, shoved a knee in my back and pulled on my shoulders. I felt my spine crack, then I rolled exhausted, onto the floor.

I was in a small mud-floored chamber with a dirty mattress and posters of American superheroes pinned to the wall.

By my side was Khady, a beautiful Diola tribe girl who worked at the house I was looking after. We'd travelled together to the provincial capital of Ziguinchor to try to connect said house to the electricity grid and to collect her identity card.

The trip was unsuccessful. The man at the electricity company – who was working hard in his hammock when we arrived – said he'd been too busy to complete the connection. Definitely next week, though.

"Okay, great, see you next week."

"*Inshallah*," he replied. This translates as "Yes, if God wills it". But in real terms it meant that we might have electricity in the next few months or we might not.

If I were a betting man I'd have tended towards the latter.

As for Khady's identity card, that took a further two years.

The masseuse was named Tierno and he was a *marabout* – a West African Islamic holy man who is a kind of shaman, sometimes known as a witch doctor. Tierno was also Khady's brother-in-law. The previous evening, she and I had been on a local bus when a tyre burst, causing us to crash. We were up front near the driver, who was drunk, and everyone was screaming as the top-heavy vehicle swerved from one side of the road to the other. I felt an odd calm knowing that I had a slim chance of surviving this crash. It wasn't so much my life flashing before my eyes as a satisfaction that despite the mistakes, the struggles and the disappointments, I had lived my life my way, mostly happily, and in a way I was proud of. I was ready, which is not to say I wasn't shitting myself.

That evening, after the crash, I crouched in the dark and ladled water over myself to wash off the diesel, dust and blood. I felt Ibrahima's *gris-gris* around my neck and when I returned to the house, voiced my cynicism. It hadn't worked; the gris-gris was nothing but superstitious nonsense.

"Of course it worked. You were the only person to walk out of the crash without even a scratch, weren't you?" Khady replied.

As the crash occurred, the bus skidded on its side for a few hundred metres as everybody screamed. The windscreen popped outwards and I clung to the side window, holding Khady with my left arm for as long as I could before being jolted off. We both fell on the driver.

As we slid to a stop, I felt the warm wet spray of diesel in my face and heard a cacophony of moans and groans. Khady was dead; I was sure of it. I went through the motions of dragging her out, panicking as I thought the whole bus would blow – a Hollywood fallacy, of course. Thankfully, she came around and we were able to assist others to safety.

Apart from my emergence without a single scratch, there were a couple of other remarkable things about this accident. First, we were only a mile or two away from a military hospital, and the medics arrived within minutes. Second, Khady's uncle lived minutes from this military base. In hindsight, the latter fact seems less remarkable – it doesn't matter where we are in the province, Khady will always be related to somebody there, often someone useful like Tierno. My bag was lying in a bush about 15 metres away. It had been ejected through the front window. I am writing these words on my laptop, which – along with my camera – was in that bag and survived as unharmed as myself.

At this point, Khady and I could barely communicate through language, but we seemed to understand each other perfectly. Tierno had finished roughing me up and she indicated that he was going to give a reading. These procedures are important after a near-miss with death. He carefully unwrapped a dirty cotton cloth, tied at the corners. Out fell a collection of beads, shells, old coins and bones.

He threw them into the dust, raised his fingers to his temples, closed his eyes and made a pronouncement. Khady translated.

"You will have a child in Africa."

I laughed. "Yeah, right." I had tried to have a baby for nearly 10 years with my ex-wife back in England, and had reached the point where I figured it just wasn't going to happen. I was cool with that. Although I'd have liked a family and the experience of being a dad, I also loved travelling and my freedom. Besides, Khady and I were only just beginning to make tentative steps towards a relationship, and at that point everything felt way too crazy to take seriously.

The date was 31 March, 2011.

A NEW LIFE

Khady and I walk along a sand track with our son strapped to her back. There is not a cloud in the sky and the sun beats down as we shuffle along trying to keep in the shade of the cashew trees. Abruptly, Khady halts, beckoning for me to do likewise. Ahead, crossing our path, is a strange creature – a chameleon, almost luminous green in colour – with an alien head and an odd circular motion to its limbs. Without missing a beat Khady pulls out a breast and with a deadly aim, fires milk at it.

"What the …?"

"If I don't offer it milk, our son will grow up to look like a lizard," she explains.

Clearly I have a lot to learn about life in Africa.

31 March, 2012

Khady woke me from a deep sleep. Bleary eyed, I pulled together some belongings and guided her, groaning, towards our Land Rover. It was 3am. We set off down the deeply rutted sand tracks through the dark forest towards the small village clinic. I parked and Khady leaned against the truck, clearly in agony.

"Simon, it hurts. Help me, help me."

I plunged into the darkness, knocking on doors until I found and woke up Ndoumbe, the midwife.

After much deliberation, Khady and I had decided to have the baby at the maternity ward in the local village. Ndoumbe had impressed us and the ward had been recently fitted out by a French philanthropist. When I say "fitted out", this meant it had basic equipment and a fresh lick of paint, not new incubators and so on. They just had three light bulbs wired in above a bench.

It was mostly me doing the worrying; Khady was casual about the whole affair. It turns out that women have babies all the time in Africa. In the event, she started labour both in the middle of the night and 10 days early, so even had we made the decision to go to a European clinic in neighbouring Gambia, we'd never have been there in time.

Forty minutes later, a little boy popped out. A wriggling blue slimy thing who, after a few minutes, turned surprisingly white.

The previous day, Khady had been swimming in the sea and running up and down the beach. I had to stop her from carrying a 20-litre water drum on her head. African women are strong. In Africa, having a baby is, well, just having a baby.

A little later while looking back through my diaries, I realised that the date was 31 March – exactly one year to the day of Tierno's premonition.

Khady Mané has always been strong. I first met her when she was working at a house I was staying in. I saw her folding sheets and as she looked up she gave a huge grin that lit up her face. For the next week, she was a distinct and silent presence that I felt inexplicably drawn to. She had no formal education, but a wisdom and presence lacking in many people I've met who have strings of degrees, and she spoke seven languages.

Although English was not one of the languages she spoke, we seemed to instinctively understand each another. When the house owner asked me to look after her home while she visited Europe, I leapt at the opportunity. Khady and I quickly became firm friends, but it was the bus crash that jump-started our relationship. I resisted at first as I felt like a burnt-out husk, unable to ever care or love again. But there's an African proverb: "Wood that has burnt once is easier to set aflame," and one day I realised I never wanted to leave.

Khady was born in the Casamance province of Senegal in 1981 during a period of upheaval and war. Like many people here, where birthdays aren't generally celebrated, she doesn't know her date of birth. When she finally renewed her identity card, she gave her birth year as 1991, knocking a decade off.

When she was a young girl, her father moved his two wives and 14 children to Dakar, the Senegalese capital. He worked as a mechanic for a French company, and brought his children up well. Senegal, although independent since 1960, was colonised by the French and still retains a strong Francophone influence, including the language, which is used in politics and education. The Casamance, 300 miles south of Dakar, is cut off from the rest of Senegal by the Gambia and hence the local Diola tribes have long wanted their independence.

Three of Khady's siblings are married to Europeans and she tells me they are "sought after" because they are direct, honest and were taught to marry for love. Senegalese women tend to have a reputation for a healthy interest in money and a visa to Europe. While Khady would like to visit, she has a strong sense of her heritage and no wish to live anywhere other than here.

African children are often passed around the family and Khady was sent to her aunt, who promised to educate her but instead made her work throughout her childhood – washing, cleaning and scrubbing from dawn to dusk. In-between, she had to cook for 20 people. Consequently, Khady never attended school. She later confided in me that the same aunt told her that I was just a source of money to be sucked dry.

In that time, without her aunt knowing, she taught herself six new languages on top of her native Diola – French, Fula, Sera, Wolof, Mandinka and Creole. She saw her mother during this time, but not her father. He was very angry when he found out Khady had not gone to school.

Khady's great passion is traditional dancing and as a young woman she was a professional, joining a dance troupe called Casadamance at the age of nine. When she was old enough, she left to tour the country with them, including long-term residences on the highly touristic coast to the south of Dakar. They were invited to perform in Europe, but disbanded due to power struggles within the group, much to her dismay. I've never seen her perform professionally, but occasionally she'll let rip at a *djembe* party. It's an impressive sight.

Having spent several months in Abene, I went back to England with vague plans to return, and then rapidly slipped back into Western life. But Khady was never far from my thoughts and we spoke whenever possible. The African rains were by now so heavy that telephone communications were often down for a week or more at a time. When we did actually connect we could barely hear or understand each other. Although we could by now communicate reasonably well face-to-face with our odd French-English *mélange*, on a crackly long-distance line it was a different matter.

Before I had left Senegal, Khady's pregnant sister had told me that if her baby was a boy, he would be named "Simon Fenton". So during one conversation with Khady I enquired about her sister's health. Khady misunderstood me and said that yes, she was pregnant. *Khady* was pregnant. How did I know, she wondered, not realising that I didn't?

"Did the Gods tell you? Are you a devil?"

"No, no, I was asking after your sister," I stuttered, my mind reeling. "Oh, never mind about that now."

Khady was pregnant! My initial feeling was of joy and relief. In fact, I couldn't wipe the grin off of my face and I was sure I could hear my heart thumping. But had I really understood correctly? Had she really understood me? Perhaps we were in fact discussing her sister's baby or some other family member – there are babies everywhere in Senegal. What should have been an ecstatic time became a confused mess. After several nerve-wracking phone calls over the next few weeks, I was about 75 percent sure I was going to be a father. Damn the crackly lines and damn, I needed to improve my French. I was only absolutely certain four months later when I returned to Africa and saw her growing figure.

Aside from my joy levels now running at 80 percent (on the Fenton scale, that's still nearing ecstatic) due to impending fatherhood, no longer did I have any difficult decisions to make about what to do with my life. I'd left it to chance and the decision had been made for me. I wasn't just deciding to go back and do the right thing out of obligation. Doing the right thing was forcing me to do what my beating heart told me I really wanted – something that I may have been too scared, or too worried about what others might have thought, to have ever done otherwise.

I later realised that I'd only opened myself to the possibility of that chance because that was what I truly desired. I wasn't entirely sure where I was heading, but I've always thought that if I can see past a challenge, then the challenge isn't big enough. Somehow and sometime soon I'd go back and support Khady. We'd have our baby and build a life together.

Khady lived in Abene, a small rural village full of artists walking to the beat of the drum, situated on the Atlantic coast of the Casamance just a few miles south of the border with Gambia. With its endless beaches, lush forests, fertile soil and friendly people I could quite easily see myself living there with my new family. And I couldn't wait.

There were hurdles to overcome, of course. Not least telling my family. They've always wholeheartedly supported me and encouraged me to live my life my own way. But I'd never before declared that I was off to live in a mud hut and have a baby with an African woman who I had known fewer than six months and who they had never met. On an uncertain income. (More than three years later and having visited me, they're on board with the idea.)

Besides having the decision made for me to move to Africa, I was happy at the prospect of actually becoming a dad. In 2005 my first wife, Mikaela, finally became pregnant. For three months we read baby books, told those close to us and investigated the prices of prams. All of our friends were having babies and it was what we wanted more than anything.

Then we went for the three-month scan. Mikaela lay there as the doctor slid the probe over her belly and I held her hand. Then I felt her hand squeeze, glanced at her face and saw tears. No words were needed – the doctor's face said it all. The baby had a chromosomal abnormality, Edwards

Syndrome – one of those one-in-several-million chance things. Even if she had been born, the baby wouldn't have survived more than two or three days.

Sometimes, events in our own lives are mirrored by those in the wider world. One day we were wildly happy, travelling up to London to have the scan. The city had just been awarded the Olympics and everyone was in a jubilant mood. The sun was shining. We were having a baby. Then, as we learned our bad news, London was hit by terrorist attacks. Looking back, this experience was perhaps one of the nails in the coffin of our relationship. We drifted apart until one day we couldn't remember when we'd last been happy together.

I fell into a new three-year relationship after that, and although we didn't set out to have a baby, neither did we take any steps not to. We decided to leave it to fate and, probably for the best, nothing happened. I concluded that it was probably not meant to be. Although part of me craved to be a father, an equal part relished my freedom to travel and live the life of a bachelor. Well, that's what I told myself – until my happiness upon hearing Khady's words revealed my true feelings.

This jubilation was all very well, but I also had to think about what I would do in Africa. Khady was adamant she wanted to stay in Senegal. It was unlikely she'd be able to land herself much more than a menial job in the UK, or perhaps teach dance. My career had reached a plateau and was ready to start a descent, unless I took radical steps.

At that point, quite frankly, I'd lost interest. I wanted family, community, adventure and to nurture my creative side.

In my twenties I'd worked for the private sector and in my thirties in social enterprises, trying to make the world a better place. Now, recently turned 40, I needed to follow my own passions and do something for myself. I'd always loved photography and wanted to pursue it professionally. This would be difficult in the UK and especially in Brighton, where every other person seemed to be an artist and photographer. Perhaps Africa was my chance, where I could take images of extraordinary things. I also wanted to write. So I could write a blog, sell articles and images, host tourists, lead tours, run music-and-photography workshops and other things.

We'd have to look at buying land and building a house, along with rooms for guests to stay in. Not only would paying guests provide me with European companionship, but would help supplement our income. I'd backpacked for years and knew exactly the kind of places I liked to stay in. I could take the best ideas from around the world and create an ideal spot to relax; a base from which to explore; a centre for culture and the arts, as well as a personal retreat for a world-weary man wanting to get away from it all and write his first novel.

It was all starting to look like an exciting – and more importantly – realistic proposition. In Africa, I would only do things I enjoyed and wanted to do. I've noticed that when I do that, the money follows.

I tried to discuss this with Khady but rare was the occasion I could get through on the phone. On some occasions I became quite distraught at the thought of her in her parents' remote village, cut off from the world and with no access to decent nutrition or medical facilities. I decided to book a trip to Senegal to check that she was okay. We could discuss the future and perhaps look at plots of land to make our dream into a reality.

I flew back with the package tourists to the Gambia, which is much closer to our home village, Abene, than to Dakar. I had been telling Khady I would come but hadn't been able to give a date. Then, finally I called and said: "I'll be there on Monday."

"Is it true?"

I could hear her sobs of joy.

There are so many stories in Africa of white guys sowing their seeds and then never being heard of again. Despite my earlier promises, she was never entirely certain. Until now. There are also stories of white Europeans being tricked into returning because of a baby and then when the baby is born, it is black. Although we both trusted each other implicitly, after a long separation with limited communications, doubts creep in. Many of my English friends, who'd never met her, wanted me to exercise caution. Given some of my previous romantic experiences, this was perfectly understandable.

I left Brighton early, exhausted, with a cold, and slightly worried about whether I was doing the right thing. Several hours later I was flying over the Sahara, transfixed by its emptiness and full of memories of having crossed it by land a year earlier. As the tourists around me played with their iPads, I tracked my route past the High Atlas, the dunes and escarpments of Mauritania, across the Senegal River, the dusty Sahel and finally the estuary of the River Gambia, before descending across white sandy beaches, clusters of rusting corrugated-roofed buildings, and the occasional mosque.

One man at Customs recognised me, flashed a grin and said, "Welcome home". I've made many journeys into the Gambia, and they are often eventful. I've had two marriage proposals from officials and made several pen friends. You don't seem to get that at Heathrow any more.

This time, I'd arrived loaded up with solar chargers, torches, two cameras and two laptops. I set the beepers blaring and was whisked off to a small room, where a rotund Customs woman gave me a sheet outlining the tax I was due to pay.

"If only I could have one of these torches," she said as she gave me a bill for around £100.

"Maybe you can," I offered.

"No, no, that's against the rules."

We discussed the problem for some time and I offered a few solutions. Eventually, she believed my pale lie that I had only £5 in cash.

"So what will we do?" she asked.

"I could give you the £5 and walk out of here?"

"Okay. Next time bring me a torch."

"It's a deal."

I was met by an older Senegalese lady called Diatou and her driver, who fired up his car using a screwdriver. Diatou is my African "mother" and source of much advice as, not only is she very knowledgeable about local culture, but she has also been married to a white man, Tom. When Khady and I had visited the town of Ziguinchor, we'd travelled there with Diatou and Tom. Khady and I were involved in the crash on our return, but tragically during their stay in Ziguinchor Tom had died. It really was a bad trip.

Diatou and I drove down through the Gambia to the Senegalese border, stopping briefly to change money with Mauritanian traders in a market. We turned off the road and travelled through villages where crowds of kids chased the truck shouting "*toubab*" (white man). Then we drove towards a swamp fringed with lush jungle and teeming with birdlife. A troop of monkeys played on the road as Bob Marley played on the stereo. It felt surreal having been on a train crossing the misty Sussex countryside just a few hours earlier.

I called Khady who said she'd meet me at Diouloulou, the town near the border. We arrived and after 10 minutes I saw a motorcycle approaching. There was a girl on the back in a long, flowing orange gown. It was my girl and she definitely had a bump. It was a relief to know I hadn't misunderstood those crackly, long-distance phone conversations. Now I really was home.

Five months later, we sat in the concrete room that is Abene's maternity ward. Our boy was swaddled in brightly patterned African cloths and we were receiving a steady stream of female visitors. Khady is of the Diola tribe, and according to their traditions, no men – including a baby's father – must view a baby until seven days after it is born. Khady was happy for me to break that rule.

We had decided that the baby would have an English and a Senegalese name. If it was a boy, the English name would come first, and if it was a girl, the African name first. Khady suggested "Rambo". (Action films are popular here in Senegal.) I talked her out of that and we named our boy Gulliver Bassirou. Bassirou is the name of my good friend who brought me to Abene and introduced me to Khady. Sometimes people ask me why I, a lifelong traveller and bookworm, chose the name "Gulliver". Well, I thought it would sound cool with the Senegalese-French accent.

One of the advantages of the African family system is the help you receive at times such as this. For our baby's first two weeks, the family rallied around to help and I barely needed to lift a finger. I really did have to fight for my right to change a nappy, as it's not something men do here.

If you go to an average Senegalese family home, there can be up to 20 kids running around. Kids of four or five years old are already caring for and carrying babies on their backs. There's none of the preciousness of the West. Kids wander around eating worms, playing with knives and chasing chickens. Of course, there's also a much higher rate of sickness and mortality. I hope that, by taking the laid-back African approach while keeping a keen eye on the wee fellow, giving him nutritious food and decent medical care, we can have the best of both our worlds.

There is a lot that Europe can learn from Africa and other developing countries about childcare, and vice versa, of course. One of the biggest differences is that I'm not surrounded by stuff or advice. Gulliver has a few toys but not too many. He has shown zero interest in them anyway and is far happier playing with a lemon or an onion. There's plenty for kids to play with and do here. We had two of his cousins with us for a couple of weeks, aged five and two. When I tried to show them *Madagascar*, a children's film, they refused to watch it. They preferred to amuse themselves outside, running around and playing in the dirt with bits of wood. There's a money-saving tip in this: save the cash for education.

Like all new parents, I felt a bit lost at the beginning. I had one childcare book, but I quickly relaxed and went with the flow and that seems to work. If it's possible to do this in the West, I'd certainly recommend it. Fashions come and go and I've been reading about various theories from the past few years that have already been discredited. All you can do is what you feel is best and it probably will be. You'll never be perfect and accepting that will be beneficial for you and the child in the long run.

I tried introducing a feeding schedule, but Khady ignored what I said and just fed him when he was hungry.

It worked fine. Many of these things are designed for the parents' convenience in a busy Western work culture and that's not applicable to us. When I asked her about postnatal depression she seemed confused, then said women don't have time for that in Africa. The reality is that new mothers here are always surrounded by people, and life continues much the same. In England, the mother has nine months of attention while pregnant, a week or two of attention once the baby arrives and then that's it. The dad goes back to work and she's left at home alone with a screaming bundle of joy for days on end.

Having said all that, the African family is the hardest thing for a toubab to get his head around. There's always someone around to help, but the cost is a loss of privacy and the sense of individuality that we Westerners prize so highly. Khady and I seemed able to find a reasonable compromise, having both family time and time to ourselves because of the support we were given.

Trying to work out who's who in an African family is like trying to unravel a large bowl of spaghetti. With men taking up to four spouses, there are many siblings around and it seems every other person is introduced as a brother or sister. Usually a brother turns out to be a cousin, distant relative or close friend; it is very confusing when you're used to taking these things literally. When I visited a local village, my friend N'ssa introduced at least 15 older men to me as his father. Then there are "Le Petit Papas", which I gather to be uncles or family friends who take a particular interest in a child, like a godparent.

Families are large. They need to be to account for the high infant mortality rate and to provide heirs to look after elderly members when they grow old in this land of no pensions, social security or savings plans. Visit any household and the kids will be the ones fetching wood, pulling up chairs, making tea or running to the shop for sugar. Children are very respectful, and any adult will discipline them if they are mucking around. Meanwhile, the old folk sit back and enjoy a rest after a long, hard life.

For the first week, Khady and Gulliver had to stay at home as no Diola man was allowed to see the baby. On the seventh day, the village chief and elders arrived, along with a *griot* couple. A *griot* is a traditional praise singer who attends ceremonies. They know the histories of the local families and attend all the important ceremonies. In the book *Roots*, after Alex Haley had traced his lineage back to a small family on the north bank of the River Gambia, the local *griot* sang the family's history back to him, allegedly confirming much of Haley's research.

The *griot*, Bouley, played *kora* (a West African harp), while his wife sang and hassled us constantly for donations. Nobody had invited them; they just seem to know about every village birth. I suspect they have an insider at the hospital. The music was lovely, but at this time of new financial pressure, I was feeling less enamoured with this local tradition.

Gulliver's head was shaved in the traditional manner, blessings were made and then Bouley announced his name in song. I'd also been offered an unofficial local name. Thinking through the various options, I decided that Chérif (pronounced Sheriff), had a certain ring to it. So Khady now calls me Chérif Mané, using her own surname.

Following the ceremony, we were free to leave our home to travel. Khady was keen to visit the local marabout for Gulliver's gris-gris protection. A very old woman in a small local village took him and massaged him with shea butter (known locally by the French term, *karité*), a cure-all potion that is rubbed into the body any time something is wrong. A marabout made him a tiny cloth-sewn gris-gris which – along with a small bottle of herbal medicine and a pouch containing his umbilical cord – were tied around his neck.

The following week, we held a party for the family and local people. Although I had wanted it to be small, people announced it around the village and soon it became a free-for-all. This is a totally normal practice in Africa.

In preparation for the party, I went to the city with Bassirou, the friend after whom Gulliver was named, to see a man about a goat. On the edge of town, we found a tented area where robed men displayed their animals. Negotiations began and very soon I was the proud owner of Geoff, a large black-and-white male. He rode home on the roof of our Land Rover. We also bought rice, onions and an entire sack of sugar to make traditional drinks, among other things.

I don't think people in Abene believe me when I tell them that a small bag of sugar, perhaps 250g, would last me a year in the UK. That barely lasts a day here. There's a big diabetes as well as a tooth decay problem, not helped by the fact that the only dentist in a 50-mile radius is a man who only had one month's training.

On the Friday, our verandah was filled with local women who came along to help, peeling onions, making sauces, sweets, drinks and so on. The party began around 7am on Saturday. Yes, you read correctly: 7am on a Saturday morning. The village elders arrived again along with the *griot* who'd spotted a second opportunity for extortion. A DJ played popular Senegalese hits and when the music was over, people chanted, danced and drummed on water containers.

Little Gulliver soon got used to the constant noise and attention of African society. He slept through most of the day. The parties aren't for the child in question, but for the community and as a way to display wealth.

As Senegal is a Muslim country, the main drinks were tea and *bissap* (a sweet red juice made from hibiscus), while I drank what I call *bissap Anglais* (red wine). Geoff was very good indeed. I was invited to sit under a sacred tree and eat his liver. The next day we ate what some say was a tasty goat's head soup.

Along with the general process of becoming a father, I was also discovering the local traditions. Every culture has its own traditions for childcare, some that we can learn from and others best ignored. A few ideas in the Casamance and Diola culture are just plain odd, if harmless.

For example, babies tend to hiccough a lot. Whenever this happened with Gulliver, Khady pulled a few threads from the cloth he was wrapped in, chewed them a bit, then stuck them on his head. The hiccoughs generally stopped, although I suspect they would have anyway. We used washable nappies, but had some disposables for when we were out and about. When I went to throw these on the rubbish fire, everyone looked horrified and told me not to. They believe that if you burn a nappy, the baby will get diarrhoea.

If you cut a baby's fingernails he or she will become a thief. When Gulliver started scratching himself, to everyone's horror, I cut his nails. Babies are given bead necklaces that they wear tightly around their necks. As Khady explained to me, she doesn't want Gulliver to grow up with a droopy head.

People don't take their babies out at night, for fear of dangerous spirits and genies. Sometimes, after a full day working on our land, we would fancy going to a local restaurant. Khady was fine with bringing Gulliver – as long as we wrapped him in blanket after blanket for protection.

One that made me chuckle was when Khady insisted on licking Gulliver's feet. This was to help him learn to walk faster.

I have to remember that some of the traditions here are no odder than the things we do in the UK. When Gulliver's hair was shorn during the naming ceremony, it was wrapped up in a piece of material that was tied around his wrist. My mother also kept a lock of my baby hair. Mind you, she didn't keep my umbilical cord tied around my neck for six months.

When I mentioned to friends in Africa that in the UK some people have superstitions about breaking a mirror, walking under a ladder or the number 13, everyone thought that was hilarious. We all believe what we want to believe.

I was of the opinion that if I went along with these small things, it would be easier to argue with the more extreme tribal traditions, such as circumcision, particularly if we later have a girl. I hadn't counted on one of Khady's first requests, though – cutting his tongue. I'd never heard of this tradition, but here, the Diola cut the little flap under the tongue. If it is not cut, they believe the baby will grow up unable to speak properly.

I put my foot down on this one and explained that the majority of the world, to my knowledge, manages to speak perfectly well with intact tongues. Although not a believer myself, I use the argument that God made us perfect and it's not good to make changes unless there are medical reasons, or unless you choose to inflict something upon yourself.

As for the circumcision, it is expected that a boy will be cut. I've heard various explanations of why most Africans perform this, one of which is that the foreskin is a feminine body part and needs to be removed for the boy to become a man. In a similar way, a girl's clitoris is considered masculine, which is why more than 80 percent of Casamancais girls are circumcised[1].

It's very difficult to say anything about female genital mutilation (FGM) as a foreigner, and especially as a foreign white male. Change needs to come from within the African societies themselves, from organisations such as Tostan, which sends trained Senegalese women into remote villages to discuss and to engage people in debate with an ultimate aim to end the practice. Organisations such as this have led to the abandonment of the practice in 5,000 communities, and Tostan is aiming for Senegal to become the first African nation to completely abandon FGM.

Fatou, Khady's sister, wishes her three daughters to go through the ceremony. When I expressed disapproval she laughed and told me I had no culture, which is frustrating – FGM has only been in practice for a few generations by the Diola. This backs up my theory that organisations such as Tostan are the most powerful way forward. Although I recognise that male circumcision is not the same as FGM, I am still uneasy about putting my son through it. There is a risk involved in Africa, and there are fatalities. For something I see as cosmetic, that to me is an unacceptable risk.

According to local tradition, circumcision is required in order to take a wife. The cutting itself is only part of a wider initiation ceremony, which in Diola culture is called *bukut*.

[1]According to a 2005 Demographic and Health survey, 28 percent of Senegalese women between the ages of 15 and 49 have been subjected to FGM. This increases significantly in the Casamance, where 94 percent of women are cut in the eastern region and 69 percent in the Ziguinchor region.

All young Diola men, whether in the Casamance, Dakar, Paris or wherever they are in the world will return to their ancestral village for the *bukut*, which occurs once every 25 years. Those that don't attend are not considered part of Diola society.

The *bukut* ritual is thought to have existed since at least the 12th century and before the arrival of European colonials, was the only formal method of education. The ritual prepares young men to take their place in society and to defend it. An entire generation of men are initiated into the tribal secrets and by this token, obtain the status of adults. Preparation for the event takes several years and the ceremony itself includes days of dancing, eating and drinking, involving hundreds of cattle and tonnes of rice.

Due to the Islamic influence, cow sacrifices have replaced pigs and milk is offered to animist shrines, usually a sacred tree, instead of palm wine. Whereas the ceremony used to last two or three months, due to the modern pressures of work and education, this has been reduced to a few weeks.

The early converts to Islam, current Iman's and missionaries have all protested against the pagan *bukut* ceremony. But rather than abandoning it, instead the Diola consider the *bukut* the most authentic expression of their cultural heritage.

Consequently I do worry that by being uncircumcised, Gulliver will stand out and not be accepted by the community, but as a *matisse* (the French term for mixed race), he'll stand out anyway. A few months after Gulliver's birth, Khady's cousin circumcised his own boy. The wound wouldn't stop bleeding and became infected. For a week or so, it was touch-and-go whether he would survive. Since then, Khady has been adamant she won't put her own child through that risk.

Despite situations like this one, many comment that people seem happier in developing countries than in the West, and most of my anecdotal experiences confirm this. Well, if you have nothing and have never had anything, you only have the present to think or worry about. I think modern Western life has stripped away our ability to be in the now. We're too busy thinking about some imaginary rosy future that might never arrive, or worrying about what has already happened.

I'm trying to be mindful of all of this with Gulliver. Kids are happy with whatever they're doing – playing with a stick, in a stream or climbing a tree, which is kind of where I'm regressing to. As adults in the West, we bombard them with "How was your day?" "What did you do?" and "Did you enjoy it?", beginning the conditioning that "now" is the least important thing.

Each day in Abene, I just try to enjoy every sandwich, every cup of coffee, watching the birds, playing with my baby. On the whole, I'm feeling happy.

TOUBAB

Life in an African village feels like being on a different planet. Having grown up with so many images in the media, I thought I'd know what to expect but I doubt anything can ever prepare you for the reality. Old men in robes stare into the middle distance; women chatter and carry goods in bowls on their heads; children, all orange with dust, screech around my feet, shouting "toubab" and falling over each other. The roads are strewn with old plastic bags and animal droppings. The streets are made of sand, so it's hard to know where the earth ends and the buildings begin. Scrawny-looking animals wander freely, often into dwellings. All this is illuminated by the shimmering white glare of the African sun.

Every day I hear the sound of drums pounding their rhythms. It is as much a part of the backdrop to Abene as the chirrup of insects at night, or the cries of "toubab" during the day. "Toubab" is traditionally shouted by children at white people. I usually shout "African" back at them, for my amusement and their bewilderment. The theory I've heard is that in colonial times, kids asked white men for "two bob" coins, hence the term.

Greetings are important in Africa and a typical one could

include a mixture of Arabic, Wolof, Diola, Mandinka, English and French along with the local Rasta patois:

As Saalaam Alaikum ... Alaikum Salaam

Na ngn def ... Mangi fi rekk

Kassumei ... Kassumei kep

Kori tanante ... Tenante

Bonjour! ... Salut!

Nice huh? ... Oui, nice, tranquil.

Toubab!

People in Senegal speak several languages and often during the same sentence. The old colonial language for Senegal was French, which is still widely spoken. Wolof is the major African language of the country; the Wolof people originate from the North around Dakar. Khady, a Diola, would tend to speak Wolof with a Mandinka speaker before she spoke French.

The Diola are centred in the Casamance and parts of Gambia and are believed to be the oldest inhabitants of the region, preceding the Mandinka and Fula peoples. There are eight dialects of the Diola language, some unintelligible between each other.

Fula are a tribe with a language spoken across West Africa. Traditionally a nomadic people, many Fula still tend cattle and are business savvy.

Mandinka is a major tribe and language common throughout the Gambia and Casamance region and the dominant tribe in Abene.

Mauritanian immigrants run many of the shops in our village, communicating in Wolof. Arabic is taught at Koran schools but not widely spoken.

Finally, in Abene there's a smattering of English due to the proximity with Gambia. It's not quite English as I was taught it, but I can generally get by.

The English have a reputation for being terrible at languages and I am no exception. When I arrived I spoke a little school-level French. When people complain I haven't learnt their language, telling them that I speak conversational Vietnamese hasn't really helped. My excuse is that I can't possibly learn all the languages of the world and they only have to learn their own and English. I've been practising French and Diola since arriving here, and now Khady and I rarely have a problem understanding each other.

There's no such thing as a typical day for me in Abene, but there are certain routines. If I awaken early, I'll sit in the cool early-morning air and watch the sun rise above the trees. Mornings start slowly with freshly squeezed orange juice. The typical local breakfast is a French-style baguette with chocolate spread, margarine or mayonnaise. None of those ever appeal and I will usually eat our home-grown tomatoes, still warm from the sun, along with a few home-grown lettuce leaves, an egg from one of our hens, and a simple dressing of oil, mustard and garlic. I've always been interested in self-sufficiency, ever since watching the TV show *The Good Life* as a boy; a friend of mine calls me Tom Good gone troppo. I even spent a weekend at River Cottage[2], learning about pig butchery. Now I live in an Islamic nation where pigs are sacred. Isn't it funny how life turns out?

In the UK, it would be very difficult to achieve these dreams without making many sacrifices. Here it is entirely possible to grow the majority of your own food, especially vegetables, salads and fruit. We have many chickens, two ducks, pigeons, rabbits and a cow. There are murmurings of acquiring a goat.

One of my earliest childhood memories is visiting my grandparents (who lived near Oxford) and helping my Granddad tend his tomatoes. The smell of home-grown tomatoes is one of nature's best and is missing in the strangely uniform red balls from the supermarket. I remember whilst in Italy, watching a friend selecting ugly green gnarled tomatoes.

"In Italy we choose the ones that'll taste the best, not that look the prettiest," she remarked.

Besides, I detest supermarkets and there is a simple pleasure in being able to reach out and pluck them from the

[2]*The Good Life* was a popular 1970s sit-com about Tom Good, who along with his wife, attempts to live a self-sufficient lifestyle in a London suburb; "gone troppo" is Australian slang for "gone crazy". River Cottage is a cookery school and more recent cookery/lifestyle television show, which also focuses on growing your own food and living a sustainable life.

shade of my verandah in the morning, with the same smell as my Granddad's green house wafting over as the sun starts to warm the plants.

Occasionally I even collect honey from bees' nests, with a little help from my friend Bakary. Recently, he led me to a nearby tree that had collapsed. A large nest was inside the trunk and a swarm was buzzing around cracks through which they accessed their hive. Bakary lit a fire underneath, then poked burning twigs into the cracks before blasting into the trunk with an axe. He wore a long sleeved coat with hood and a sun hat. The bees, understandably in my opinion, weren't especially happy and swarmed all over us. As I'm wont to do, I stood still, grinning like fury. It's when you panic that they sting. I have faced down a charging gorilla and gangsters in Shanghai, so I don't let bees worry me. Soon, Bakary was pulling out great chunks of dripping honeycomb with his bare hands. He handed me a piece and I bit into the warm smoky honey. It doesn't get much better than that.

As yet, we don't have running water so hauling water out of the well for our fruit trees and flowers is a big job. A single banana plant needs 40 litres a day and we have 15 trees. We're also growing guava, mangoes, avocados, pineapples, oranges, lemons, mandarins, grapefruit, custard apples, passion fruit, onions, beans, bananas and more. During my twenties I worked in farming and I have always found manual labour therapeutic, a great time for thinking. Sometimes I get so lost in the rhythm of the work that I finish whatever I am doing and start going around again. I start early in the day as by about 10am it is far too hot to do anything but lie fanning yourself and occasionally mopping your brow.

There are plenty of other tasks to complete as I water the trees. I nip new buds from the trunks of orange trees, concentrating the growth upwards. I pick up any rubbish and deposit it in the relevant space – something the Senegalese find hilarious. Having said that, recycling does generally happen, for example if I throw away an old pair of flip-flops they'll turn up somewhere else pretty rapidly. Old tyres turn into shoes and old bicycle chains become gate hinges.

I spent much of my twenties living and working in Vietnam and this Asian experience toughened me up, making me used to dealing without the everyday things we take for granted in the Western world. For the first year in 'Nam I lived remotely and had no phone. This was in the days before everybody had a mobile. I used to travel 12 miles every week to the village, where I could call home from the post office. When my truck was destroyed by a buffalo, I had to go on a Russian Minsk motorbike. When the monsoon came and roads were too muddy, I'd travel on a buffalo and cart. (That made it onto my CV for a while and helped land me a job.) Eventually, we had a telephone mast installed by the Vietnamese army and I had an antiquated Russian telephone exchange in my living room that looked like something from an early Bond film.

The first time I arrived in Abene, I didn't think there was much here. One main street with a few shops, all selling the same items, and a lovely almost empty windswept beach.

I later discovered there are more than 4,000 inhabitants and the village sprawls into the bush in all directions. Things happen all the time. On one occasion, a nervous rumble was spreading throughout the village. Kids screamed and everyone, the young and adults alike were running to take shelter, barricading doors and windows and keeping quiet. I was pulled into a shop.

"*Fat-fat* (quick)," said Khady, pushing me inside.

"Ssh!" she replied as I asked what all the fuss was about.

I peered through the slats into the dusty street to see a flash of red. A masked devil creature flitted across, brandishing two machetes. I felt as if I was in the horror film *The Village*, where similar-looking creatures terrorise a village deep in the woods. Not for one minute did I think I'd live through the same experience whilst watching that film at a Brighton multiplex.

It was the Kankourang.

"If you're not good, the Kankourang will get you," parents warn their children. There was genuine terror about and when I went to have a better look, I was dragged back into the darkness. I had heard about the Kankourang, but presumed it (or them – no one seems quite sure how to refer to the Kankourang) to be ceremonial and wouldn't actually hurt anyone. A friend had some sharp words with me:

"You have Khady and a baby, don't be stupid."

"But I know karate," I said, like an idiot.

"Okay, well just so you know: a tourist was severely beaten up a couple of years back and the Kankourang have machetes. The police won't do anything; nobody will do anything. You are part of the community now so you have no excuse. You need to take these things seriously."

That told me. I learnt that the Kankourang are masked people of the Mandinka tribe who issue warnings and provide social order to a village. For instance, if kids pick mangoes before they're ripe, disturbing the year's harvest, the Kankourang will come and teach everyone in the village a lesson. If you keep out of their way they won't hurt you. If you move towards them or take a photograph, anything could happen.

They tend to be present, in force, during children's initiation ceremonies. These initiations happen once a year, when older women cut (in the FGM sense) younger tribeswomen. One day there were many Kankourang's around Abene, causing businesses and even the school to close for the next couple of weeks. Khady explained that girls were being taken from the bush – where they'd been cut – to the sea to wash in salt water, which is good for the wounds. The fear generated by the Kankourang means that whenever they are in an area, there will be few people on the streets. Although part of the local tradition and done with full parental consent, cutting is technically illegal, so the presence of the Kankourang allows this practice to continue undercover.

Local people, police included, believe the Kankourang to be a genuine spirit, not some guy in a Chewbacca suit. Although in the cities there are moves to ban them from hurting people, it'll be years before that trickles down to the villages.

By now, the Kankourang had moved down the street and I ventured out. From a safe distance I saw it walking towards a procession of dancing women. One man taunted it and wouldn't move. Maybe like me, he knows karate. The Kankourang struck him to the ground and beat him. I was too far away to see how serious the situation was, but the man lay there for some time after the devil had gone, then got up, dusted himself down and wandered off.

It's not uncommon to witness traditional ceremonies and I'll often follow the beat of drums to find out what's going on.

One day, the beat was accompanied by hundreds of kids running around looking scared. It was near Frederick's, a local bar filled with Rastas who usually can't afford a drink. It was beer o'clock, so I bought a cold one and stood on the verandah to see what was happening. Frederick explained that there was a ceremony in progress, where several men were possessed by the spirit of *Simba* the lion.

Their muscular bodies were oiled and covered in leather gris-gris and cowrie shells, their faces painted like lions. Their purpose appeared to be to terrify the kids, who were stampeding and screaming in absolute terror. They had good reason: one of them was caught and given a huge whack across the back. An old woman danced, legs wide apart, thrusting her pelvis forwards. Women in cheap dresses with straight wigs approached me smiling and I realised they were men.

"Why are they dressed as women?" I asked.

"Because that's so funny."

"Oh, right."

Then I heard a hushing sound through the crowd. One of the lion men was approaching me. Kids crept away. Everyone watched the toubab: what will he do? The lion man growled, pawed at me and then stuck a six-inch nail up his nose. As it happens, that's one of my party tricks, so I just smiled.

There was a sigh of relief from the crowd. The toubab was strong.

The other occasion that I saw the lion man was when watching *lutte*, which is West African traditional wrestling. Wrestling was big in England in the 1970s and I remember watching it on Saturday afternoons with my Grandma. I even spent a short time working for one of its biggest stars, Big Daddy, but despite this I wasn't much of a fan; it was always more theatrical than sporting, in my opinion.

The fighting seems real enough here. Wherever I go, I see lads practising in the sand. Alongside football, wrestling is the most popular sport in the country and the biggest *lutte* stars are, like footballers in the UK, multimillionaire idols. After a recent match on television, a roar went through the entire village and then youths zipped up and down the main sand drag on motorcycles, beeping horns and generally being boisterous.

Lutte will normally start as the temperature cools down in the late afternoon. On one occasion, as a warm-up, a *Simba* dancer minced around like a camp feline Michael Jackson. In fact, that whole event was fairly homo-erotic, the wrestlers' bodies heavily muscled, soaked with sweat and wrapped in leather cords holding the ubiquitous protective gris-gris.

Drummers thrashed away on the edge of a sand circle. Wrestlers between matches took a break from flexing their muscles and pouring water on each other to dance with *Simba*. Amidst this, opponents fought each other at a fast pace, with the occasional break for officials to make dull speeches. The crowd lapped it up, cheering and occasionally breaking into the circle to dance to the drums alongside the fighters.

The crowd roared with delight as, in a cloud of dust and spray of sweat, the winner hurled his opponent to the ground. I looked up in time to see hundreds of bats pouring out of a single tree, flying off into the jungle as yet another spectacular sunset spread across the skies.

I straddle a fine line between immersing myself fully into the local culture and retaining my British sensibilities.

Life feels a little dull when I go back to England, although that's partly because I have no purpose there any more. At the same time there are many things I miss about European life whilst in Africa.

Many people tell me they want to see the real Africa. For some, it's vast wilderness, safaris and Maasai warriors, but that's not the reality for the millions of people eking out a living here. I suppose the real Africa is that of the villages, cities and townships. Extended families with lives governed by jealousy, religion and superstition, tranquility suddenly erupting into extreme violence, extended greetings, smiling kids, lack of privacy, corruption, bureaucracy, heat, harsh landscapes and disease.

I suspect many British people would not want to live as I've been doing, without electricity, the threat of a local beetle that causes foot-long blisters, picking maggots from my feet and having no other coffee but Nescafé – that's the worst thing. Every day here is a battle against the dust and dirt, much like it must have been in Europe a hundred or more years ago. The interface between ground and house is minimal. The chickens stroll through the house, sometimes defecating along the way.

We don't yet have a fridge, vacuum cleaner or washing machine, which means daily trips to the market, regular sweeping with a few twigs bunched together and lots of hand washing. Anyone with children will understand how much washing we have, especially without disposable nappies. But compared to local people I lead a life of luxury. I'm sitting and writing this on a laptop. I have a book to read. I can buy a coke if I feel like it.

Sometimes, my friends tell me I'm an African now. Then, as was the case when I went to Guinea, I was offered a free room that was so dirty and squalid I ran to the nearest hotel. Checking in, I felt bad realising I couldn't put up for one night what is the reality, day in day out, for millions of people. Or I'll be squatting around the dinner platter, eating communally with my hands feeling like I belong here, then everyone talks together in Wolof, Mandinka or Diola – often all three – so fast that I'm lost. Some communication is non-verbal and I'll probably never understand it.

No matter how I feel I may be able to empathise with people, I am automatically distanced, simply because of people's perception of me as something utterly different. Khady tells me that often local people think white people are devils; I know that sometimes she suspects I am one.

One tradition that does perhaps link the English and the Senegalese is their love of tea, although I'm not fond in either its British or African incarnation. The local tea is taken as incredibly strong shots, like a tea version of an espresso. Often I'll bump into a friend sitting by the roadside taking part in the tradition that happens all over the Sahel. Boys and men will be hunched around a small, chipped enamel teapot, which is perched on a couple of lumps of charcoal.

Attaya, the local tea, is more than a drink. The process of making and drinking takes an hour or three and is time for chat, gossip and discussing the football. Everybody tells me that it is the drink of Africa although the tea itself is Chinese and the process imported by Arabs from the North.

Green tea is added to a small enamel pot with some water and an equal amount of sugar. Once boiling, a shot glass is filled from the pot from a height of at least a foot, often two feet. I've only ever see one person miss. That was me. The tea is poured back and forth between the glass and the pot many times before being returned to the fire for a while, then the shot glass refilled, again from a great height. The last time I watched I counted 30 pours, which can take an hour or more. The tea is dark green and frothy. You can almost see the tannin.

The pot is refilled with water and another glass of sugar, using the same tea leaves, and the entire process is repeated. Then it is repeated again for the third and final serving, by which time the tea leaves are spent.

The first cup is strong and bitter. This is for death.

The second cup is sweeter but still strong. This is for life.

The third and final cup is very sweet and the one my palate can stand. This one's for love.

When the heat subsides slightly in the late afternoon, I'll often head to the beach, sometimes having a beer at Ibby's shack, often over a large platter of freshly grilled fish, prawns or lobster straight from the ocean. Floating in the warm sea is a time to relax, to lie back and just exist. The life of everyday clutter I lived in Europe has disappeared. No rolling news, bills, junk mail, cold callers, reality television or other "conveniences" of the modern world. Or what I call the "buggeration" of life.

Here there is just daily life: chatting to friends, staring into the middle distance, blowing on a fire, eating a sun-warmed tomato, watching a parrot, growing my own food. The past and the future don't seem important; there is only *now*.

On September 11 2001, I was in a Hindu temple on top of a mountain, wondering whether to have my head shaved. At Tirupathi temple, this is considered auspicious and they raise money by supplying the wig industry, largely for African-American communities in New York. It was a day or two before I found out about the terrorist attacks. I spent the next year in Eastern Africa, so I didn't see the video footage until the first anniversary.

It's not so easy anymore to stay out of the loop, with modern communications that have made their way even to Abene. I once remember meeting a chap who changed his flight at the last minute, stayed in Borneo and disappeared into the jungle for six weeks. When he returned, he discovered the flight he should have been on had crashed. His family spent six weeks in agony, having been informed he wasn't on board but sure there must have been a mistake as he hadn't called. So, I suppose it's largely for the best that communications have improved, but it does take away a little of the magic sometimes.

I'm a reluctant mobile phone user and only bought one so that I could contact other people, not so that they could contact me. I've had some amusing situations, such as the time I was wandering along the beach when an insurance salesman called me on my British number.

"Hi, this is Wes, calling about your insurance."

"Sorry, I won't be interested."

"Don't worry sir, it'll only take a minute."

"But I told you I won't be interested."

"It's about your contents."

"I don't have any contents."

"Oh, (sounding confused). How about car insurance?"

"Mine covers me from Mauritania to Nigeria for 30 quid. Can you beat that?"

"Err, let me ask my manager ..."

At that point I hung up.

As darkness falls, candles are lit and we gather around a huge plate of rice, vegetables and fish, eating communally. Anybody without a chair squats. Using our right hand we eat quickly. It's invariably rice with a sauce, like *yassa* (onion and lemon), *maffe* (peanut) or a slimy green substance (*bissap*) that has the texture of pond slime, but tastes better. Occasionally, a portion of meat that would typically do for one in Europe, will be divided amongst us. Normally there is fish, which is more plentiful. Khady tears up the flesh with her hands and flicks it around, usually sending the choicest morsels in my direction. Visitors often join us, but no extra food is cooked. We simply divide what's available amongst those present. The dogs wait for the leftovers and what they don't eat goes to the chickens.

Here's a recipe for *yassa*, my favourite Senegalese dish, which can be made with fish or chicken.

Chop 4 or 5 large onions and the same number of garlic cloves.

Crush a handful of peppercorns with a jumbo cube (or chicken stock).

Stuff a little of this into each chicken quarter or fish (1 per person).

Heat vegetable oil and fry the chicken or fish for 10 to 15 minutes on each side until crispy.

Crush the onion and garlic with the rest of the pepper, another stock cube and a pinch of salt. If you don't have a large African-style pestle and mortar, a food processor will do.

Meanwhile, cook rice as you normally would.

Remove the chicken or fish from the oil and place to one side. Add the onion mixture and a large mug of water to the remaining oil in the pan. Bring to a simmer for a few minutes, then return the fish or meat, cover and leave for a couple more minutes.

Then add half a cup of lemon juice, a large dessert spoon of French Dijon mustard, and salt. Adjust the quantities to taste – it should be very tangy and have the Opal Fruit factor that makes you suck your cheeks in a bit. Simmer for another 5 to 10 minutes.

Serve on a large platter of rice. All gather round and eat from the same plate, with your right hand if you dare.

A delicious summer alternative is to grill the fish or chicken on a barbecue. For added authenticity, turn off the lights and cook by candlelight, using the glow from a mobile phone for the tricky bits.

Most people in Abene don't have televisions. Often it seems like people are just sitting, not doing much, but it's more complex than that. Once, I stayed at my friend Bass's compound in Ziguinchor. After I'd greeted about 40 people, showered African style and plastered on the mosquito repellent English style, we went to sit on a bench outside a small shack selling not a lot with Phil Collins playing on a tinny radio. Surprisingly, he's a musical hero across Africa. I've met ultra cool rappers who, when they find out I'm British, ask if I know Phil.

Maybe this is the real Africa, sitting, watching. With Bass, people stopped to greet us, sometimes staying long enough for a café *touba* – the ultra sweet local coffee that is heated with a herb to give it a liquorice-like taste. Taxi drivers stopped to ask directions. A lad asked for help filling in a government form. Bass told off some kids who were misbehaving; any adult will discipline any child here and the kids respect the elders. Life happens on the street and it was interesting watching it unfold in front of me.

In the UK, we often don't know our neighbours or socialise with them. But something rather wonderful has happened in my neighbourhood in Brighton for the past five or so years – Zocalo, named after a Mexican tradition. On a specific

Sunday evening in summer, we are encouraged to switch off the television and bring a chair, or even a sofa, out onto the street to sit and chat with neighbours and passersby. Being British, at the allotted time, I looked out of the door to see business as usual, except for a couple of others nervously checking out what was happening. After a while though, conversation and wine flowed and everyone had a great time, all of us wondering why we don't do this every week. It seems a shame we need to organise an event to do what is natural across much of the world.

In Abene, we'll sit around the fire where Khady plays *balafon* (African xylophone) and I tap a rudimentary beat on a *djembe*. Or we'll go to a reggae party or to watch some live music. It's possible to see live music most days, whether traditional sounds at a ceremony, a reggae band in a sweaty club or a *djembe* group. Most of Senegal pulsates to the furious beats of *mbalax*, a highly rhythmic Afro pop popularised by Youssou N'Dour.

As we leave the house, we'll hear the beat and follow it down pitch-black sandy tracks through palm groves, almost deafened by the chirp of insects and croaking of frogs. We'll arrive at a bar where a sound system has been set up and a collection of Rastas and guys dressed like '70s pimps, groove and skank around sandy dance floors. If we're lucky, there'll be some drumming.

This isn't a tourist show, as there are usually very few toubabs around. The spectacle of several drummers pounding beats and kicking up dust – sometimes with a dancer on stilts – is awesome. Sometimes there will be a rapper. On the slower numbers, rather than wave a lighter, jesters light an end of an aerosol can, spraying it towards the crowd. Health and safety has some catching up to do in Africa. One thing I've noticed is that as the gig progresses, they stop singing into the microphone as invariably they're miming.

Whatever the music, people will dance. A woman will throw herself against the rhythm, bare feet pounding up the dust, body thrust forward and knees almost reaching the chin with outstretched arms flapping, like a lunatic bird attempting to take off. The energy is intense and is kept up for a few seconds or maybe half a minute, before she'll fall back into the crowd laughing, only to be replaced by another. Complete and utter abandonment and unreservedness with no hint of the aggression that might accompany such intensity elsewhere.

I DREAM OF AFRICA

I am hanging onto the back of a motorcycle, slithering through mud. Paddy fields, shacks, pigs, kids. A girl, barely into her teens mouths "me love you long time". A toothless man appears, something round his neck. A python. More people surround me with cobras, green mambas – all pushing closer.

"Mine tasty friend." "Mine make you strong." "Mine make you harder."

The snakes brush against me, wriggling against my neck, down my shirt. I can't stop them: they're in my eyes, my ears, my nose, crawling into my mouth. I am drowning ...

I wake thrashing and sweating back in Brighton. The snake wine, a decaying cobra pickled in rice wine bought near Hanoi years ago, sits near my bed, still open. Never again. I smash the bottle.

It's time to go back to Africa.

I became obsessed with Africa as a boy, an obsession that never ended but matured from boyhood fantasies to an interest in the political realities in the 1980s and then the culture and people when I finally visited. However, I was quite a shy boy with little travel experience. Had someone told me that I'd end up living in an African village I'd have thought them mad.

I can put my initial interest down to a number of factors, not least of which was an obsession with Tarzan that, along with lapping up the books, television shows and films, involved swinging on ropes from a bridge over the local dual carriageway. Our neighbours, an elderly RAF couple called Chip and Helen, told me stories of elephants, monkeys and crocodiles whilst being stationed in Rhodesia, which enthralled me. When my mother, who worked at a local college, was visited at home by African students wearing traditional costumes, the obsession heightened. Ethiopians, Gambians, Zambians and Malawians. Friendly men with friendly smiles told me of their lands where it never snowed. I couldn't believe it.

I was 22 years old when I went off to travel the world. I knew no one who'd travelled beyond typical British holiday destinations. If young people were taking gap years I hadn't heard about it. Kids at my school left at 16 for apprenticeships or youth training schemes. I had romantic images of hitching across Europe, buying a camel to cross the Middle East and perhaps getting a job as a cabin boy to cross an ocean somewhere. In a bookshop I asked for a book on travelling the world. They pointed me to the *Lonely Planet* guides. I thought "ooh, where shall I go?" India was the first book I set eyes on.

For the next two years I travelled throughout the subcontinent, across China and south-east Asia on a shoe string. After earning some cash in Australia, mainly by picking apples, I journeyed home across the Karakoram highway, zigging along the Silk Road and zagging back on the legendary trans-Siberian train. Occasionally I'd be on well-established backpacker routes, but more often I was travelling alone with just a backpack and a smile.

The first time I set foot in Africa was in the mid-1990s. Driving south from Eilat, a developed Israeli resort, into the Sinai peninsular, I arrived in the desert with the turquoise waters of the Red Sea to my left and the rusty mountains of Saudi Arabia across the waters. I stopped at a shack where a Sudanese man sold drinks. There was an outline of Africa painted on the wall, filled in with reggae colours. I was gutted not to be travelling further south.

A few years later, when I thought I'd met my Jane, we visited Africa proper, this time for a year. We climbed volcanos, hiked through steaming jungles, swam in lakes, went on safaris, tracked chimps and gorillas, canoed in dug-outs to the beat of the village drum and camped wild for eight months. Apart from a spooky encounter with an aardvark, I loved every minute. We returned to England, travelling the long way around. I had married Mikaela in Vietnam and we decided to settle in Brighton following our African adventure.

I had always struggled to correlate the life in my head with the real world. I wanted to live life passionately, travel, have adventures, do meaningful work, spend my time doing things I love with those I love. I couldn't get my head around working 48 weeks of the year to pay off a massive debt, but thought maybe I was the odd one, so took steps to try to normalise my life without losing sight of my passions.

I started working with a charity and before long was running a social enterprise, offering work to various disadvantaged groups in London. It was highly rewarding when people moved on positively. Less so when they died, or simply disappeared, most dramatically when a South African employee hanged himself during rush hour at a Canary Wharf tube station, or an East European was poisoned and crucified. After our attempts to start a family, Mikaela and I had drifted apart. Ironically, she wasn't ready to settle and still yearned for the travelling life, moving back to Africa. So she went. My head was still in England and focused on my career. We had a lovely home in Brighton and a group of friends that I wasn't ready to give up.

I met someone else and fell head over heels again. Like someone on a treadmill who couldn't jump off, I again committed matrimony. This could have made for a happy ending had she not already been in a relationship with someone else. I fought for a year to save the marriage but it was never the same and one day she was gone, too, leaving me devastated despite what she'd done to me. In fact, it was probably a combination of grief of the two relationships failing in such quick succession that made it so hard to bear.

Unable to focus on my career, I started a temporary job with the council. One day, a "client" asked me for a knife to kill himself. When my colleague asked him if he wanted a serrated or smooth blade, I realised I probably wasn't tough enough for the job. I was dealing with dirty needles, diarrhoea, murder, someone attempting to chop their hand off, someone else overdosing on nail varnish mixed with orange juice, and smells I didn't ever want to know the source of. Possibly not the best environment for somebody dealing unsuccessfully with his own personal problems.

Then, when I thought things could sink no lower, I slipped and fell down the stairs, breaking my foot. I'd been heading down to open a bottle of wine. I lay alone in the dark for an hour, winded, in agony, unable to move and staring at the bottle just out of reach. I was at one of my lowest points; I seem to need these to kick-start massive change. I believe that if you are unhappy, you have three choices: remove yourself, do something to change the situation or accept it totally.

It became clear what I needed to do. I needed to challenge myself and live my passions: Africa, travel, adventure. I called into work to say I was now well and would no longer be coming in. But before reaching paradise it was necessary to cross a desert, both physically and metaphorically.

BLEAT, PRAY, LOVE

There are times you think life can't get any worse. Then you discover you're halfway across a minefield. I am deep in the Sahara. I am lost, freezing, confused and upset. I wrap my head in a Tuareg scarf to keep the warmth in, the sand out and so that no one can see my eyes. I am not exactly in the middle of nowhere, but reckon I am not far away. I can barely communicate, I have no idea where I'll end up tonight or whether I'll eat. I take a walk into the sand dunes and should the wind change, the people nearby may hear the long howls of an animal in pain.

I arrived in Africa at the end of January when it was cold and wet. Specifically, Fez in Morocco, the largest Islamic medieval city in the world. Over *harira*, a thin breakfast gruel, I was offered several guides by my spectators. Hamid was a short fat man with a walrus moustache who produced more mucous than a camel. He took me in his wreck of a car to the opposite side of the city, from where we slowly walked back. It seemed little different from the times of the Arabian nights: goats heads, pointy slippers, ornate tea pots, pulsating and wailing Arabic music, the smell of spices, cooking meat, perfumes and drains.

Although I was there and took it all in, my head and heart were still back in Brighton. I had needed to get away, but was I doing the right thing? I wasn't sure. Just one day away and I was lonely, jealously watching romantic European couples on their weekend city breaks. It was too late to turn back and I knew deep down that I needed to make this journey. I'd been scarred by my experiences, but I didn't want to be crippled by them. Movement seemed important.

Later, whilst wandering around the medina in Rabat, I was joined by a "friend" who insisted he didn't want anything, then later got angry when I did not give enough. He showed me through some old streets and into a private house with a fine view across the city. It was here that I hit a slick of bird shit that may as well have been ice. I went up into the air horizontally, landing on the small of my back. I was winded and could barely walk. I had a sore back for the next few weeks, which is not so great when you know you have thousands of miles of rickety buses ahead. As I limped out, the house owner demanded an outrageous fee for the privilege.

I took the Marrakech express via Casablanca late in the evening, arriving to find a flea pit on the edge of the vast Djemma El-Fnarr Square with its snake charmers, food stalls, musicians, three-legged monkeys, storytellers, beggars and lunatics. After a day of exploring the souks and monuments, I was perking up and ready to move on from the beaten track and on over to the ditch.

The bus south through Western Sahara was a 24-hour journey, giving me plenty of time to think and wallow in my sadness. I was upset, angry and confused, not quite able to believe what had happened to me. But slowly as the trip progressed, my state of mind improved. I started to feel excitement about the journey as well as curiosity to what the future would hold. The Moroccans on the bus were the first I'd met who were not trying to sell me something. Instead, they ordered *tajines*, olives and drinks at the various stops and wouldn't let me put my hand in my pocket for anything.

We crossed the mountains and the next morning, I awoke in desert proper. It was flat, desolate, full of camels and with a cliff drop into the Atlantic on the West. At Dakhla, we passed stunning turquoise lagoons full of kite surfers. The town itself was an urban mess. I met and chatted to many Senegalese and Guineans, mainly about if I could help them with a British visa. The answer was, and is, no.

From here on, there weren't many buses. There wasn't too much of anything actually, and so I took shared taxis that squeezed us in like sardines and covered vast distances cheaply. I left the following morning, crossing the tropic of Cancer and down through the desert to the Mauritanian border. The scenery changed constantly, with scrub, bleached out sand dunes, gravel plains and even fields of rusty red flowers.

After the border, we drove into no man's land; a bumpy rocky track where we were overtaken by a herd of camels. Mauritanians emerged from the haze with their distinctive blue robes, from which they pulled wads of cash for exchange and phone credit cards for sale. It is fair to say that Mauritania was one of the more challenging countries that I have visited. Despite being twice the size of France, many people I spoke to had not heard of it and certainly couldn't place it on a map. I mean people back home in the UK – the Mauritanians had heard of it, of course. I didn't know much myself, just that it is well known as a country where slavery still exists. Although this was made illegal in 1980, there are thought to be around 100,000 Mauritanians still enslaved.

I stayed with a guy called Mohammed in Nouadhibou, a dusty junction town in the featureless desert and the main settlement in the north of the country. Everything was shabbier than Morocco. The cars were wrecks, reggae booming from their sound systems.

Every day, the two-mile long iron-ore train winds its way from Nouadhibou to the mine deep in the Sahara, near the Algerian and Malian borders. There is one dilapidated passenger car or you can travel free of charge in one of the iron-ore containers. I opted for a seat so that I could take photographs, but all the padding had been ripped away, leaving bare metal to sit on. The windows were too grimy to see through properly, much less photograph the scenery outside. My fellow passengers ignored me, the only white person onboard. They gossiped between prayers, where they knelt on the floor, murmuring and mysteriously rubbing themselves with pieces of black rock.

We trundled along at a pace slightly faster than walking, crossing sand and gravel plains until darkness fell. I drifted in and out of sleep but it was cold, dust blew through the carriage and the train jolted continuously, sometimes violently. Still sore from my slip in Morocco, every bump passed painfully through my body. I was aiming to get off at the town of Choum, which according to the guidebook, you could not miss and is where most people alight.

At 2am, we started slowing. I saw no lights or signs of life. A couple of people jumped off, a truck revved, turned its lights on and pulled away. I was half asleep and figured that couldn't possibly be Choum. Twenty minutes later the guard wandered down and I asked him how long till the town?

"*Derrière*," he said, waving his hand back.

A chill ran through my battered spine. Thinking quickly I decided to get off at the next stop and to attempt to hire or rustle a camel to take me back. There are no roads in this area and I'd been told that the end of the train line was deep into alleged Al Qaeda territory and off limits to foreigners.

Alas, it wasn't until the sun rose, turning the sky into a raspberry ripple, that we reached the next stop. The end of the line. I reached the end of my own personal line when the fellow bunking above me tested every ringtone of his phone between 4 and 5am.

We were at the iron ore mine where the police arrested me, partly to ascertain whether I was a spy and partly for my own safety. I resolved that it could have been worse, although I wasn't sure how.

I was popped into a shipping container, where a little man, Mohammed, hunched over a charcoal burner brewing tea. We sat, smiling at each other for most of the day. I was questioned by the police a few times. Three months later I spent some quality time drinking local spirits with Liberian fishermen in a shipping container-turned-bar. Shipping containers are like buses: you wait all your life for a go in one and then two come along at once.

At the end of the day, the *gendarmes* reappeared and stuck me in the back of a jeep. We scooted around the town, back and forth, picking up other people. Then we drove out across a piece of desert. I noticed a great tangled roll of barbed wire and a wooden sign with a large "MORT" in red letters (French for "death"). It was a minefield.

Despite previous holidays in Cambodia, Afghanistan and Vietnam's DMZ zone, this was a new tourism experience for me. But this was a thoughtful minefield; old tyres marked a route across the sand and as long as you stayed within a few metres of them you were safe. That didn't stop me having a mild anxiety attack, though. I'd come to sort my head out, not have it blown off.

I sat, at the "train station," for several more hours, surprised at how cold the Sahara could get. This station was even more remote than Nouadhibous' station. In fact, there was no station. Just 10 people and a pile of luggage by the track. We stood like hitch hikers, waiting. And waiting. Not only had I gotten lost but here I was, confused and upset in the middle of the Sahara and I was freezing cold! Not only that, but it started spitting with rain. Surely it couldn't get any worse?

Hours later a train arrived and we hauled each other, and some goats, on board. I settled into a carriage where I met my first friendly Mauritanian, a young guy who was building telephone masts and spoke about 20 words of English, which is enough for me to chat for a few hours. He shared some goat's milk and when we passed Choum, accompanied me off of the train to make sure I didn't get stuck in an endless iron-ore train yo-yo.

Quite frankly, when I saw Choum I decided not to be too hard on myself for missing it the first time. There was no road, no electricity, just five or six shacks built around a central dust bowl. It was 2am and I was taken into a shop. The shop keeper, Mohammed – yes, they're all called Mohammed around here – told me it was forbidden by Islamic tradition to turn away a stranger in the night and led me next door to a room with a dirt floor and a bunch of snoring goat herders. He indicated a bed in the corner, but judging by its fragrance and shape, it had only recently been vacated by a camel. So I bedded down on the floor in my sleeping bag, making sure to set my alarm for 4am when the (once a day) public transport left for Atar, my destination.

I didn't hear the alarm. I awoke with a start, checked my phone and saw it was 6am. The goat men had left. Once again, I was filled with dread, thinking I had to wait another day for the truck to Atar. Fortunately, this being Africa, transport rarely leaves on time. The truck was still loading up and there's always room for one more. I piled in and was soon racing down sand tracks as the sun rose, sometimes just following the vague marks of the previous vehicle. We crossed a plateau, went through remote villages with thatched beehive-shaped huts and eventually saw a grove of palm trees and the town of Atar. The driver, Mohammed, beckoned me to his sister's shop, who gave me coffee that tasted like she'd brewed the dirt from under her fingernails.

We were close to some desert towns with ancient Saharan history and spectacular landscapes. Mohammed explained he'd take me in his jeep and I simply had to pay him several hundred pounds for the privilege. I walked out laughing manically and instead headed towards the garage. It seemed it was going to be difficult to explore further without plenty of time or enough money to hire a four-wheel drive. I was hungry, exhausted, hot and dusty and couldn't remember my last shower. I'd almost crossed the Sahara. This was supposed to be a break. I started thinking about the tropical paradise of southern Senegal and decided there and then, no more desert. I needed greenery, cold beers and a beach.

So I took a shared taxi to the Mauritanian capital of Noakshott for the final leg of the journey, stopping at a nameless two-goat town. My first meal in three days was a plate of greasy yellow rice mixed with goat sphincter, tubes and fat. Now, don't get me wrong, I'll happily eat onion rings, calamari rings or even spaghetti hoops. But goat rings were a circle too far.

Noakshott was fun, and I finally ate well in a Lebanese restaurant. It was a short taxi ride with what can only be described as psychedelic Sufi chants blasting to the point of distortion, to the Senegal River which forms the border between Mauritania and Senegal. A small boy poled me across the wide expanse of water in a dug-out canoe.

Despite having by now spent so much time in Africa, Senegal was a revelation: a riot of colours, sounds, smells, history, wildlife and super friendly people, bar the occasional rascal. Within half hour of arriving in the nation, my taxi was forced to the side of the road as dozens of black four-wheel-drives passed and I caught a glimpse of President Wade.

I rehydrated in Saint Louis, a lovely island town with crumbling French colonial architecture that reminded me of Hanoi. Then, after a couple of days exploring Dakar, I wound up in a cramped bus bound for Ziguinchor in the Casamance, which was still part of Senegal, but with the country of Gambia separating it from the North. My neighbour on the thin wooden bench where I was so squashed in that I was only able to rest one butt cheek at a time, was Bassirou Diallo, a tailor and singer-songwriter. We talked and he told me of his home in Abene. I decided to visit.

It wasn't plain sailing. We arrived in the Gambia as the sun set, crossing the river on a ferry and then continuing into the Casamance. Due to past troubles, there is a military presence and roads are often closed by 8pm. This happened to us, just an hour or two before reaching the provincial capital of the Casamance, Ziguinchor. We were in a tiny village with one small shop lit by a candle. It had no food, bar sweet biscuits. I lay my sleeping bag out in the sand by the roadside and slept, unlike the other passengers who had no such luxury and crowded around a fire all night. They had the last laugh as I was woken up by a goat licking my face.

At 8am, tanks rumbled past (always disconcerting in a poverty-ridden African state) and the road opened again. We continued on our way as parrots swooped overhead and monkeys raced across the road, hooting.

After my journey across the bleak, lonely desert, I had found paradise. Abene is a small village on a beautiful beach, full of Rastafarians[3] and the beat of the *djembe*. Bassirou took me to an artist's house, where a local Diola girl called Khady worked. The artist wanted a European man to look after her house whilst she returned home for a few months. A few months where I would be able to rest, think, relax and slowly rebuild myself.

As one door of my life closed, another opened.

---

[3] They're not true Rastafarians as they mostly practise Islam and are actually *Baye Fall*, although they look like Rastas, play reggae and say, "Yes, aye" a lot.

THIS IS AFRICA

It's steaming hot and mosquitoes buzz around my ankles. I'm besieged by money changers, phone credit sellers, drink sellers, cashew nut sellers, everything else sellers, people trying to carry my bag, taxis reversing erratically, everyone screaming that their car, their bus is faster, more comfortable, will leave sooner. Eventually my taxi is ready and we crawl in.

I look around and tick off my mental "bush taxi check list": cracked windscreen; wires ripped out; door doesn't close; years of dust and crud; ripped upholstery; live chickens on the floor; distorted religious chanting on the stereo at ear-splitting levels; window winder handles missing (the great African mystery – where do they go?); exhaust hanging on only by a bit of dangerous-looking wire. This is Africa.

Ever since the movie *Blood Diamond* which featured the phrase, I've heard people saying "This is Africa" as a response to anything bad happening. And I've also heard it as a response to anything great happening. Quite frankly, things are rarely in the middle, and that's the way I like it. I agree with one of my musical heroes, Neil Young who once said: "travelling in the middle of the road soon became a bore so I headed for the ditch. A rougher ride but I saw more interesting people there."

Since when did your continent define you? I've never heard anyone say, "this is Europe" or "this is Asia". What's different about Africa? Why is the continent where man was born still the most extreme continent?

There are many joys to be had, living in Africa. Sometimes I'll be on the beach as the huge orange sun sinks into the sea, a fresh juice in hand, Gulliver at my feet, Khady by my side and a monkey playing nearby. Everyone is friendly, smiley and joyfully exclaiming "Ah, this is Africa".

Then everything goes wrong, buildings collapse in the rain, the bus crashes because it was overloaded and poorly maintained, children die needlessly of diseases we've eradicated in the West. Friendly people look concerned and state solemnly "Ah, this is Africa".

But, it's the minor irritations of life that can drive a man crazy here. As when I went to buy a car.

Following the bus crash, which was swiftly followed by several less serious but equally scary accidents, I decided I needed my own wheels. As much as I love hanging around in Senegalese bus stations, I couldn't waste hours or days on a 100-mile journey or put my family at risk.

There is a fairly healthy secondhand car market in the Gambia, where vehicles are imported by sea or driven down across the desert from Europe. Senegal has a rule that one may only import a vehicle younger than eight years. It exists for good intentions – they don't want to add to the motley collection of old bangers on the road, but the result is poor people (i.e. the general population) cannot hope to afford a vehicle and travellers driving their own, older vehicle across Africa will often bypass Senegal, thus denying much-needed tourist income. Unless you're working for an agency or a business that can afford to import a new car, you go to the Gambia to buy an older one. Living so close to the border means that I can generally get away with driving a Gambian vehicle in Senegal.

So, I went to the Gambia with a friend called Baks. He was taking me to the Amsterdam-Dakar rally car auction (although those crazy Dutch actually end up in the town of Banjul, not in Dakar). After the journey across the desert, vehicles are auctioned off to raise money for local projects in the Gambia – schools, hospitals, water wells and so on. So, the Dutch people have an adventure, the Gambia gets much-needed cash and people like me can find a cheap car. Back of the net.

The auction was set for 2pm in the main Banjul football stadium. At 8am, Baks knocked on my hotel room door telling me it was now starting at 9am. I dunked my head in water, dragged on some clothes and ran. The previous day I had withdrawn the money; a condition of the auction is you pay on the spot in cash. The largest Gambian note is 100 *dalasi*, around £1.30. I didn't think a brief case would be big enough, so I had a backpack filled with bricks of notes. The man behind me in the queue at the bank wondered aloud if there would be any money left for him.

We arrived at the stadium at 9am, but, given that we were in Africa, it didn't start till 10.30. A convoy of cars and jeeps arrived, toubabs hanging off the sides and sitting on the roof racks. There was time for a brief inspection. Baks was slightly more mechanically minded than I, although only slightly, and we picked two or three that we thought were worth bidding on. For the cheap price you are paying, you have to take a bit of a chance.

The first, a Pajero, rapidly soared way above my limit. I felt a bit depressed and anxious that I was going to be unsuccessful. In the event, the man bidding didn't have the money to pay. The last I heard was that if he didn't pay, he'd be thrown in jail. I was then outbid on a Cherokee jeep. My final choice was a lime green Land Rover. I was bidding against a well-muscled and finely coiffured Nigerian, but he wasn't as keen as I. For a little over £1,000, it was mine. A 1994 Land Rover Discovery, with a Defender engine (the best kind for Africa and they'll last forever), fitted out with beds, sink and a fridge in the back.

After paying, the previous owners congratulated me and ripped off their matching lime green T-shirts as a gift. I took photographs and christened the car "Kermit".

Next, I had to complete the registration and custom procedures. Baks offered to help and thought that registering the vehicle would take a day. Yeah right, this is Africa.

First of all, we took Kermit to the mechanics for a check over. I was sort of expecting a garage, but we pulled over to the side of the road at the turntable, Gambia's single roundabout, where a collection of wrecked vehicles sat in the sun whilst mechanics worked in the sand beneath the shade of several palm trees. They knew their stuff and over the course of a couple of days cleaned the engine (crossing the Sahara takes its toll), mended the oil filter, repaired the gearbox and clutch and a few other bits and pieces, all as cheap as chips.

Then we went to Banjul to complete the paperwork. The first stop: the den of rogues and rascals that is the Gambian Revenue Authority, to obtain a TIN number, without which I could do nothing. This is the Gambian version of a national insurance or social security number. We arrived in the morning and waited in a hot warehouse filled with rotting paperwork and lethargic officials in military garb swatting flies as ancient fans stirred the soup.

I thought it might take an hour or two. Lunchtime came and went. The officials went outside for their one o'clock prayers. I went to buy some cokes and was accosted by a Rasta who tried to convince me he was in fact the gardener at my hotel and could he borrow some cash and that he'd definitely pay me back later. Yeah, right. Later on, a Sierra Leonian importing a car told me he'd bought the vehicle with money from diamonds. By 3pm, the heat was stifling and everyone began to doze. I had a little too much to dream and came round a little to see things had taken a surreal twist as dwarfs on bikes were pedalling around selling wallets.

A boy had been running back and forth with a wad of papers, obtaining the necessary signatures and stamps. I couldn't understand why they'd developed such a complicated system where nobody seemed to know what they were doing, including the officials.

At last he came to me saying the TIN number was within reach and I simply had to wait two or three days. Unless I gave him 100 *dalasi* (£1.30). Five minutes later I had my TIN number. Great, I'd nip over to the license-plate office, grab the plates, pay for the insurance and road tax and off we'd go. "No, no, it's past 5pm," said the boy. "Everywhere is closed now."

The next day, Baks assured me that now that we had the TIN number, the rest was a piece of cake. We'd be on the beach by lunchtime. Yeah right, this is Africa.

Banjul is a pleasant West African city on a swampy island. I saw large billboards of the president His Excellency, Sheikh, Professor, Alhaji, Doctor Yahya Abdul-Aziz Jemus Junkung Jammeh everywhere[4]. One memorably read "there

---

[4]By the time this book is published, it is likely that he will have crowned himself King and added this title to the list.

is no need to feel guilty any longer if you did not vote for me." He is a remarkable man who has even discovered the cure for Aids, although he's yet to disclose this to the rest of the world.

We were back in the same warehouse with the same boy. It was a scorcher. Today we followed him around, chucking out 100 *dalasi* notes here and there to smooth the process. I counted that we went to 12 different offices just to obtain the number plates and a road-worthy certificate (they didn't look at the car, I simply gave them 100 *dalasi*).

The number-plate office itself was on the other side of town in what looked like a wrecked building. As we drove in, it felt like the kind of place where I'd be pushed out in the courtyard and await a jeep of soldiers to whizz in and gun me down. But they didn't. The office was a desk under a tree surrounded by police officers. License plates in hand, we finally went to the port where containers were being unloaded from ships and found a small office near the harbour where mysteriously I was given the road-worthiness certificate.

We were nearly done. We simply had to pay for road tax and insurance and then Africa would be my oyster. We arrived at the road tax office at 4.28pm, as they were pulling down the metal grill. Immune to the ubiquitous 100 *dalasi* note we were told to return in the morning.

The next day, according to Baks, we'd leave early and be back for breakfast, having completed everything. Yeah, right. We arrived early at the tax office, took a ticket number and queued. When we reached the front we were asked for the insurance policy, which we hadn't obtained yet. The insurance companies were in Serekunda, which on the map looked a long way away.

Baks knew a short cut and we bumped down a potholed track through small villages with children in our wake crying "toubab". Soon we were in the insurance office, and luckily, this was straightforward. I wanted a policy to cover the whole of West Africa – Mali, Nigeria, a couple of Guineas and so on. The girl offered me a price. I looked pained and she reduced it to around £30. I told her she was lovely, she blushed, I think, and knocked off another 100 *dalasi*.

We went back to the tax office, collected our ticket and were then shown to a queue outside in the sun. An hour or so passed and I chatted to a Chinese green-tea importer who sold me the health benefits of this beverage. I wandered off to a mango tree under which a lad made me a coffee.

I headed back and chatted to a Mandinka from Soma in central Gambia. He fired questions at me and was particularly interested in the birds of the Casamance. As I struggled to describe a flamingo, I was called into the office. I jumped up and stubbed my toe on a rock. Blood sprayed across the path and several people in the queue jumped up shouting "I'm sorry". One of West Africa's more endearing habits.

Once in the office, I was faced with more chaos. At last a girl saw me and interrogated me about my income and then handed me a bill for my income tax, not the road tax as I had thought. I had to go elsewhere to pay it and then back again for another form. This was my clearance certificate, which cleared me to go and pay the road tax. I walked to a different office and joined a brand new queue.

Tick-tock. By now, most people had been in a similar position to me for two or three days and tempers were short. There was a scrum of people around the window of the tax office and people kept trying to push in. I showed no emotion and no sign of impatience, my strategy for the past three days. I knew that if I showed frustration I'd be made to wait twice as long.

I chatted to Ousman, a water-filter sales representative and a local woman who'd studied for seven years at Aldgate East in London, near my old office. I asked if she missed England and she replied no. The final fee was a little higher than I'd expected and I was 10 *dalasi* short. I turned and everyone in the queue, digging deep, donated a *dalasi* each.

Ousman very kindly offered me a lift back to my guest house. As I left the area, I noticed a large plaque with the Gambian Revenue Authority's mission statement, which included the following words:

"We strive to be efficient, organised, transparent and professional."

I thought, perhaps naïvely, that once that I'd received my license plates, insurance, road tax and road worthiness certificate for Kermit, I'd be ready to go. But yes, you guessed it – this is Africa.

Baks had disappeared and I wasn't exactly sure where the garage where we'd left Kermit was. I found a taxi with a driver called Salsa and asked if he knew a mechanics' workshop on the side of a road under palm trees.

"Of course," he said and off we whizzed. Kermit was there, but I noticed broken glass on the floor of the driver's seat. The window had been smashed. The stereo, one battery and the fridge had been removed.

I was given a couple of explanations of what had happened to choose from. After a slightly frantic time whizzing around Banjul, chasing people and, as the Senegalese say, "*Beaucoup blah blah*," I managed to fix the window and got my bits back – thankfully everything had been taken to the mechanics' house for safe keeping, but that didn't explain the broken window.

It was great to drive back home in my own vehicle instead of squished up in a bush taxi. No more hours waiting at bus stations, only to spend the journey cramped up in the boot of a Peugeot as the meat in a *jaifonday*[5] sandwich, whilst

---

[5] A large African woman's bottom. An English female friend of mine was once called to be a judge at a "Jaifonday" Competition. I want that job!

being sprayed by diesel fumes and dust. However, the one downside is all the police and military check points, sometimes as often as every 10 miles. Even the men in the friendly ones wave me over just to have a chat, which slows the journey to a crawl.

At the Senegal border as I waited for my passport to be stamped, everyone suddenly left their desks, knelt on the floor and started praying to a man in voluminous robes who had just entered. He completed the prayer and they all outstretched their arms with palms faced up and muttered "*Amine*" (Amen). This man was an important marabout.

A little later I passed through a small town and was pulled over by police. They asked me for all the car documents. Then for my passport and driving license. Then for my yellow-fever vaccination certificate. It was the first time I have ever been asked for this, and for that reason I'd not thought to bring it and had left it behind in Abene.

This was a blatant excuse to extort some cash; they don't even ask for this document at the airport. I argued for some time to no avail. They wouldn't let me pass for less than 20,000 CFA (about £25). I was worried. This town was en route to everywhere I would ever drive to and I couldn't possibly pay this every time I wanted to drive somewhere. If it wasn't this vaccination certificate, the police would find something else to sting me with.

Baks was with me. He had an idea.

"Look, he doesn't have cash on him. Let him leave his driving license with you whilst we go to the bank, then we'll return with the money," he said. They accepted this whilst we drove straight to the police station and complained to the chief. Khady being more than eight months pregnant at the time strengthened our case. To my surprise the chief was angry and phoned up the police officer, demanding he return my license and let me pass. The *gendarme* stared at the floor as he passed it back to me very grumpily.

It was not much consolation, but as I drove through the town where this occurred, Bignona, I realised what a thoroughly depressing and soul-destroying place it is, and that this is the *gendarmes'* home. It's a one-horse town that reminds me of so many others throughout Africa and Asia. Lads in rags and sunglasses weld together old bits of metal. Piles of rubbish and old tyres rot in the heat. Women lethargically swat flies from warm watermelon. Tumbleweeds roll across the dust in the furious heat.

I try to let days like this wash over me. There's no point getting stressed and one must simply accept a little inconvenience as the price for living one's dream. Then, as I reached home my clutch failed, at which point I decided that although it wouldn't achieve anything, a little fist-shaking would make me feel a whole lot better.

I'm generally opposed to paying bribes, but when it's 6pm, I'm still 100 miles from home, the road will close in an hour or two due to a curfew, the baby is crying in a hot car and you can feel your eyeballs starting to sweat, it's difficult to be so high-minded. Little people like me are fairly powerless.

The only way forward is to be squeaky clean, cross every T and dot every I. As Baks said, even if you have everything, the police will ask to see your whip. You then spend several hours trying to prove that a whip is not a legal requirement. Not long after purchasing Kermit, a chubby police officer with a rumour of a moustache, asked to see the reflector warning triangle that cars are legally required to display if broken down. No problem, I thought. I have that. "Where's the second one?" Oh, bugger. This was at a police checkpoint, ten metres ahead of a military checkpoint. The soldiers sit watching who gets stopped by the police. Then you drive forward for ten metres and get hit again. Genius.

Sometimes, it's a case of breaking the tension and allowing an official to save face. Tony, my blind traveller friend, told me of a time Customs officials wouldn't allow him into Mauritania unless he gave them his stick. Eventually he offered to swap it for a camel, everyone laughed and he went on his way.

Compared to the large-scale corruption found elsewhere but everywhere this may be small fry, but it cripples the locals and inhibits development. What is "just a quid" to me is a day's wages in the local economy. This system breeds inefficiency, unfairness and lower standards. Rather than fix a car problem, chuck cash at the police and later have an accident because the problem's not fixed. The bus I crashed in was seriously overweight, causing it to roll when a tyre blew. Earlier I had seen an elaborate "handshake" between the driver and a policeman. The police were more focused on money extraction than increasing road safety; they don't care about the vehicle's safety or whether the driver was drunk.

Similar arguments hold true throughout the system. Lower quality but more corrupt businesses win government contracts. Don't worry about those troublesome environmental or health and safety regulations: just slip a bureaucrat some money. Although individual corrupt transactions may speed up processes and be beneficial to businesses or individuals in the short term, there is no evidence that tolerating corruption is beneficial to the growth of a nation.

In my experience, mainly in Vietnam and Senegal, most citizens believe corruption is so entrenched that it's a way of life; they're fatalistic about it. There are strategies for its reduction, but, like just about everything it is complex, otherwise it wouldn't still be happening despite being an age-old problem.

There needs to be transparent leadership and good examples from the top. Salaries of officials should be raised to decent living wages, which would reduce temptation. Recruitment should be transparent and there should be good financial and audit systems. The penalties for those caught should be a serious deterrent and there should be benefits for officials who are honest. Governments must protect whistleblowers when corruption is endemic and it's difficult to speak out. There should be external independent control organisations, a free press, watchdog groups and channels for complaints made by citizens.

Right, I've solved that problem. Tomorrow I'll tackle world peace.

Invariably, just as I think I've got everything sorted, a new problem arises. After a particularly large water-filled pothole swallowed up my license plate, I drove up to Banjul for a new one. I asked for directions to the police station and slowly meandered my way through giant potholes filled with orange mud. As I cruised down one street I had that horrible feeling something wasn't right, then heard the whistle of a policewoman. She sauntered over and greeted me in that slimy way of appearing friendly as you're about to shaft someone.

After a lengthy greeting, whilst I tried not to stare at the three tribal scars on each cheek, she asked: "You do realise this is a one-way street?" pointing to a small road sign that was obscured by a broken-down truck. I explained how sorry I was, and that I'd turn around. The sign was clearly blocked and I'd not caused any damage, so could she accept my apology and let me on my way?

"But you've broken the laws of the Gambia, you've violated our road safety codes. YOU MUST BE PUNISHED!" She was now beginning to scream and I started getting worried.

"You will go to court and you will be fined 2500 *dalasi* (£50)."

"*Kassumei!*" I said: the Diola greeting.

"*Kassumei kep,*" she replied, looking surprised and immediately mellowing.

That was a bit of luck. She was a Diola. I conversed for a few minutes and explained that I was a friend of the Gambia, spoke a bit of Diola, that Khady and my son are Diola. "So, perhaps you can accept my apologies?"

"Okay. Please send my greetings to your family."

If I can't impress with language, I try to pass myself off as a harmless idiot who doesn't know any better. I usually succeed.

Everyone keeps telling me "This is Africa," in case I'd forgotten. It seems to me to be the everyday excuse that everything is always going to be a bit shit.

Of course, it is not all bad or else I wouldn't stay here. Just this morning I saw yet another idyllic village, thatched round houses surrounding a rustic well. Then a troop of howling baboons ran across the road in front of me, as if on photographic demand.

THE LITTLE BAOBAB

"Do you know how big that land is? Do you really think that price is possible," the old man says.

Khady and I are with the owner of the piece of land we love. Our hearts sink. We can't go above this price so I tell him that I'm wasting his time.

Then he makes me an offer. Nearly half the amount that I'd proposed. I counter-offer, slightly lower.

"Done."

I sit, dumbstruck. I've been haggled down!

"You have a new baby, a house to build, wells to dig. I understand toubabs – I know you aren't all millionaires. This is a good price and a fair price – for you and for me."

I waited many months before searching for the land upon which to build our home and guest house. The pregnancy, followed by a new baby, and then buying Kermit the car was quite enough to be getting along with. Besides, this gave me time to look long and hard as well as to try to understand the system before committing to anything so major.

In the meantime, we lived in a small round house beneath

a large *fromager* tree. This is also known as a kapok tree. *Fromager* is the French term, named due to their use of its wood for making the boxes for cheeses such as camembert. I had an odd experience with this tree. It was tens of metres in diameter and perhaps 30 metres high, its branches home to numerous bats and birds whilst the roots were crawling with snakes and lizards.

I approached the tree to photograph the beautiful red flowers emerging from its base. It was a sunny day, with still air and bird song. A breeze picked up as I approached. It got stronger and stronger the nearer I got. As I reached a point a few metres from the tree I was actually leaning into a wind. All the loud bird chatter had stopped. I looked up to see a single cloud racing across the sky, and then down to see a small whirlwind of dust enclosing me in a circle. I turned to go back to the house and the air became still again.

According to local belief, this tree is home to a genie; a spirit that may be good but the default assumption is that it is bad. Some Diola believe toubabs are genies and I'm not helped by my name. "Si" sounds like the Diola word for "vampire".

Whilst living beneath the giant *fromager*, we were visited by my deaf and blind friend, Tony. He preferred to sleep on the verandah, because the spare room was hot. Sleeping in the open is an alien concept to many Africans who will retire to bed with all doors and shutters tightly locked as protection against the spirits of the night. I have a constant battle with

Khady to leave the windows open during the oppressive humid heat.

"He might tell you he's hot, but that's not the reason he sleeps outside," Khady said.

"He's blind, which means he can see and communicate with the genie in the tree. If you ever ask him he won't admit to that, he'll just tell you he was hot."

Well, with logic like that, you can explain anything. Khady also told me that the genie can give me anything I wish for, but that I must pay a price.

"Would it give me money?" was my predictable question.

"Yes, of course," she replied. "But for a large amount, you must sacrifice someone you love, for example your brother."

Funnily enough, ever since I mentioned that, my brother's not come to visit.

We have six *fromagers* on the land that we ended up buying and I am constantly being lobbied to chop them down, in order to thwart the bad genie. These are very attractive trees with huge buttresses – classic jungle trees. As we're creating an eco-lodge with forest, birdlife and wildlife-spotting opportunities, it is against my ethos to cut something down when it's perfectly healthy. I suggested to Khady that since we've had plenty of good luck then perhaps we have a good genie. She's bought that argument for the time being.

Once we consciously started looking for our own land, it didn't take long for word to get around and soon everyone was dropping by to tell us about their plot, the best plot.

Although we considered elsewhere in the province, we ultimately decided that Abene ticked all our boxes. It's not difficult to see why other toubabs who have travelled across Africa decide on Abene as somewhere to settle. It has a little bit of everything: the people are friendly and welcoming; the landscapes are beautiful; the beaches are like computer screen-savers; there's a vibrant drumming and music scene with festivals and traditional ceremonies throughout the year; land and building costs are extremely reasonable by European standards. And finally, it's only one hour from Banjul international airport. I can eat, and indeed have eaten, breakfast in Brighton, England and been on the beach in Abene in time for sunset.

The cost of land ranges from laughably cheap to toubab prices, which, despite being obscenely high for here, would barely buy you a parking spot in the UK. Provided you complete the paperwork correctly, land ownership laws are robust.

Our decision came with certain conditions. Khady's Muslim so didn't like one place because it was teeming with pigs. She says they're *salty* (dirty) because they carry a worm that buries itself in your feet. That's true and she's dug a couple out of mine. Another piece of land was close to Abene airport. I say airport, but in reality it's an overgrown strip of land where cows graze and has rarely been used since the owner of the one luxury hotel in Abene was arrested for cocaine trafficking. We decided against this place in case tourism, or the drugs trade, picks up and the area is developed.

Finally, we found a spot we liked. A hectare of untouched land, not too far from the beach or the village, but tranquil – which is just as well because the name of our district is Tranquil. A friend's father, one of the village elders, negotiated for us and we reached what I felt was a good price. Then the seller, Moussa, told us a tourist had come in with a higher bid. I figured this was a tactic and held my price. Khady and Tierno, her marabout uncle, visited the land and sprinkled herbal medicines to bring us luck with negotiations.

Then something odd happened. We found out that the seller, Moussa, wasn't the seller. That's not odd as people often ask a family member or friend to sell on their behalf. I understand that and if they take a cut, we're still talking about a small slice of a tiny pie. However, we discovered that he wasn't even connected to the seller, who had no idea his land was being sold. I wouldn't have handed over money without double-checking the paperwork with trusted friends and authorities, but I was annoyed to have my time wasted.

The real owner's brother, Chérif Aidara, was an old friend of Khady's and he had spent years living and working in Sweden. Chérif invited us over to his beachside house and explained the situation. He asked me how much I had to spend and I told him the amount we'd negotiated with Moussa. This is when, on his brother's behalf, he negotiated me downwards.

We nearly had the land! Later, Khady told me that Moussa, who tried to cheat us, told her she was crazy for going to speak to Chérif and getting half the price he himself was offering. Hmmm.

Chérif gave me a good piece of advice: "Trust yourself and Khady. Nobody else. Ever. Assume everybody is involved in monkey business, including the village chief."

On Friday, having thoroughly checked things out, we arrived at the house of Chérif's brother, a professor. He was an elderly man with a shaved head, skull cap, long white beard and an ankle length blue *boubou* (robe). After some pleasantries, he took us into his bedroom. We all sat on the bed, read through and signed the papers, and counted out the West African francs. That was that.

I was eager to start clearing undergrowth from the land and think about what will go where. Exploring it thoroughly, I became even more excited. There were palm trees for palm oil and palm wine production. Mango trees. Jungle groves. Khady picked a red fruit from a tree where they were abundant. Peeling off the skin left four or five lychee-like segments that tasted of toffee.

I visited the local hardware shop and bought two machetes. It was time to work.

In the mid to late 1990s, I built a 20-hectare pig farm on the edge of a mountain range 100 miles or so from Hanoi in Vietnam. As a young guy in his mid-twenties I learnt a lot about construction, dealing with different cultures, working in a different language, management, leadership and resilience as I battled with tropical disease, searing temperatures, monsoons, snakes, car crashes, motorbike crashes, working with the Vietnamese army, corruption, bureaucracy, liars, thieves and plenty of weird mystical bullshit. I must have enjoyed it, as here I was doing it all again, albeit on a smaller scale. This time it was personal. I had a vague plan, although – this being Africa – we had to improvise as we went along.

Once I completed the paperwork I'd clear the rubbish, build a fence and dig a well. After the fence was finished, I planned to plant fruit trees so that they'd become established during the imminent rainy season. Then I'd construct a small shelter where the builders could shelter from sun and rain, install a simple African toilet and erect a small round house. The house would be somewhere Khady, Gulliver and I could move into and live for a few months whilst building the main house. Later this would be ideal for guests.

I'd need a solar system; electricity was important so I could run my laptop and do my photographic work, and here we were way off-grid. Although we could survive on well water, I'd need a system for connecting taps, possibly a bore hole which would provide quality drinkable water. Finally, once the main house was finished I'd consider further round houses and a bar.

I wanted to make everything as traditional as possible to match my aesthetics but also I felt this would be more attractive to guests. I was hoping to use mud blocks, straw roofs and minimal concrete – although sometimes I'd find myself facing a battle, when the things that I didn't desire were seen as modern and desirable.

I'm regularly told that the Diola as a tribe respect nature but if I turned my back for five minutes, they were liable to chop down my favourite tree and leave plastic bags and cigarettes strewn across my land. The notion of not throwing away rubbish hasn't really caught on, and no one seems to care about spoiling a beautiful landscape. Like much of the developing world, until recently everything came wrapped up in palm leaves or other natural products which, of course, are fine to throw on the ground. Attitudes haven't seem to change as fast as the materials have.

Once I was in a public taxi sitting next to the window when an old man handed me a big wodge of plastic to throw out, so I put it in my pocket. I couldn't throw it, despite their obvious bewilderment at the weird toubab who pocketed their rubbish. Khady saves any hair that I pull off my hairbrush, but that's for a different reason. If an enemy gets hold of it, they could perform voodoo on me. When it got so hot that I went to the "barbing salon" to shave my head, Khady collected my golden locks and wrapped them up for safe keeping.

Cigarette butts are a particular bugbear, as Gulliver collects and eats them. Telling the builders that didn't stop them, even though I supplied plenty of bins and ashtrays. Most men smoke and no one thinks twice about picking Gulliver up, fag in mouth, breathing fumes all over him. Every morning, Khady would leave the builders their breakfast – a tray of baguettes with margarine. One day I collected maybe 60 butts in one go. Fed up, I stuffed them into the baguettes. If they're good enough for my son to eat, they're good enough for breakfast, I argued. After that, the builders used the ashtrays and probably thought I was insane.

For weeks I thought about house plans and drew sketches in school exercise books. We were eager to move onto the land, but it wasn't the best time to build, as the rains were imminent. Building a small house first was one of my better ideas, as we'd experience a build and make our mistakes on a small scale. I designed a single round room, with a wall at the back dividing off a narrow strip in which was a toilet, a basin and a shower.

I drew it out on a scrap of paper, added a small verandah, indicated a six-metre diameter and said I wanted big windows. Who needs an architect?

Local houses are traditionally made with mud blocks known as *banku*, which is much cooler than cement. Windows are always tiny, offering little in the way of ventilation but are cheap and provide security. Almost everyone uses the cheap corrugated roof. I found it too hot, like living in an oven and it often leaks. I'm guessing that in most cultures, there's a period of development where people want to move on from traditional options that may be viewed as primitive. Once a level of financial development has been reached, people can focus more on aesthetics and realise traditional ways are often more beautiful as well as practical.

I'm surprised that not too much thought seems to have gone into keeping a house as cool as possible, for example the basic ventilation principles that are practised in Asia. It doesn't have to cost much, but it does seem to me that there is a way of doing things and unless somebody had some overseas experience and been exposed to new ideas, then the old ways are continued.

A simple case in point is toilets. The local system is for everyone to pee in the shower. The shower is generally a palm leaf shelter with a couple of bricks to stand on, where you take a bucket. When you walk in, you are usually faced with a muddy, litter-strewn mess that smells, well, like a dirty toilet. This is in open-air countryside areas with unlimited space, where it will take an hour or less to dig a latrine that could be filled in and moved at intervals. But this doesn't seem to be of importance or on anyone's radar. You pee in the shower. That's it. That's what our fathers did and that's what everyone else does.

Despite the toilet situation, it was fun coming up with new ideas. I thought about a *casse impluvium*, which is the traditional Casamance style of building. These are round, containing a central circular open area with a tank for collecting rain water; from above, the building would look like a donut. I also toyed with the idea of a two-storey house. Having seen the problems people, including us, come across with one-storey houses, I'm glad I didn't push forward with that one.

I also decided on a separate kitchen and bar that I christened the Jolly Diola bar (Diola is pronounced Joller). If I could persuade Khady's friend, Titty, to be barmaid I might come up with a more amusing name for it. The bar would be a wooden platform with a roof shade above the kitchen. The ideas came thick and fast, changing as I saw other houses and ideas across the region.

I thought long and hard about a name for the house and our business. Then I planted a small baobab tree in front of our house. It's currently knee height and will grow as we all grow and the land develops. Baobabs are one of my favourite trees and the national symbol of Senegal. Le Petit Baobab or the Little Baobab. Not to mention that I often called Gulliver a little baobab. I decided that was a lovely name, Khady agreed, and so that's what we went with: the Little Baobab.

With a spectacular sense of timing that few can achieve, I managed to start working and building the very week the rains arrived. I'd seen monsoonal rains in Asia, including waist-high floods in Hanoi, but my first proper West African downpour was a sight to behold.

We could hear a little rumbling in the sky before we left to go out. Khady had said rain was coming and that we should stay home. I learnt a valuable lesson. Always listen to a Diola. Women here will follow their man and do what he says, even if it's plainly idiotic. Had Khady argued with me, I'd have thought twice. So, as we sat allegedly watching some local dancing, in reality we were enthralled by the great show in the sky. The sky was almost continuously lit by spectacular horizontal sheet lightening. The rumbling got louder, the power cut off and as I looked down the track towards the village, it was as if I was staring into a vast black tunnel with forks of lightening shooting down every few seconds. Behind me was a glorious red-sky sunset, lending a surreal edge to the occasion.

It was time to leave. As I walked across the village square I was hit by a blast of wind that filled my face with sand. It howled around me and everyone was running, shrieking with what felt like a mixture of fear and delight. I was equally panicked trying to protect my camera. Then the temperature dropped by about 10°C, the heavens opened and the sky dumped on me. We took shelter and waited half an hour, before wading home along what were now sand rivers.

When we finally reached home, Khady gave me her "you stupid toubab" look and told me we wouldn't be going out in the evenings again until the end of the monsoon. It was a relief to feel the rain, as humid heat had been building up throughout the spring. Now we could expect regular cooling downfalls for at least three months. The rains end in October and then the heat builds up again until about December when the weather breaks, humidity drops and cool air arrives. The short winter is perfect – warm enough to swim in the sea during the day but chilly woolly-hat weather in the evenings when we huddle around fires. No wonder this is when the majority of tourists visit. Then, from around March, the heat starts building again and the cycle continues.

Before starting on the house, we needed a water source, so over breakfast one morning we met with Mustafa, a local well digger. When not digging wells, he wears long robes, sports a skull cap and is knowledgeable about orange tree production. He'd been recommended as a very honest and hard worker. We agreed terms and I committed to buying some cement for work to start. It was important to get moving with this before the really heavy rains began.

We wanted to be independent from mains water, not only to save on bills but because it is unreliable. The mains water in the village had been switched off for several weeks as the local water company couldn't afford to pay its electricity bill. As is so often the case, the problem is down to infrastructure and mismanagement, due to inexperience and lack of education.

We take water for granted in the West and even when there is a drought in the UK, I don't remember the taps ever running dry. Fortunately, our local southern region has not been affected by the droughts afflicting the broader Sahel region. Wells in Abene are only seven-to-ten metres deep and water gushes out, clean and clear. With the mains water off and not having a well with our rented accommodation, we were forced to walk and fill containers from a neighbour's supply. Then, by the law of Monsieur Sod, the mains water was switched back on the very same week that we moved onto our own land where again we had to haul water from a well.

We were fast approaching Ramadan, the month of fasting in the Islamic calendar. My sole experience of Ramadan to date was in Qatar, one of the Gulf States, where I spent a week with teacher friends I'd met in Hanoi. Although we ate and drank freely behind closed doors, this was forbidden in public. Even whilst we were driving in a private car, we had to duck out of sight to swig water, or we could have been reprimanded. Thankfully it's not so strict here.

There was a benefit for me this year; the workers digging the well and finishing the fence were all trying hard to finish before fasting began. They would continue working during Ramadan if necessary, but they had a good incentive to speed up. Nobody wants to be hungry and thirsty, labouring under the African sun. As I was responsible for feeding several builders, I selfishly thought I might save a bit of food money. That wasn't to be. Although people don't eat during daylight hours, they more than make up for it at night, meaning it wasn't quite the healthy detoxing month I had expected.

Between sunrise and sunset during Ramadan, Muslims do not smoke, curse, eat or drink. Not even water. I enquired whether they get up and drink gallons of water just before the sun rises but they said no, they just have a good meal in the evening after dark.

I did want to live healthily for a while though, so for that reason, and partly for solidarity, I joined in, apart from water. It was so hot and I was working, I knew I couldn't cope without fluids. Unfortunately for me though, Khady was exempt as she was breast feeding. So I had to sit and watch her tucking in.

I was told Ramadan began on Friday. On Thursday night I was alone in the provincial capital of Ziguinchor on some business, so I took the opportunity for steak, chips and a few beers before my self-imposed month-long fast began.

I felt a little worse for wear on Friday but didn't allow myself my regular coffee. I just drank water and felt hungry. There was a long wait at the bus garage. Sometimes when travelling alone it would be cheaper and easier for me to take public transport, but now I remembered everything I didn't like about this as I stood waiting in the sun feeling dizzy. Half way home, torrential rains fell and the car leaked, flowing straight onto me. I was dropped on the highway a mile or so from my house and waded home through vast red muddy potholes, by this point starving. I felt things wriggling across my feet but was unsure if it was worms or snakes.

Then I performed a classic Fenton manoeuvre. I hit a mud slick under the water and felt my legs go from beneath me. I was wearing a backpack that contained my laptop and camera. Twisting my body mid air I turned and landed on all fours, my equipment safe and my chin dipping into the water. My work tools always come before the potential for injury or broken bones.

When I reached the house, Khady was there with her friend. I told them I was starving and couldn't wait for the 7pm end of fast. They both burst out laughing and told me Ramadan began tomorrow. It's based on the lunar calendar and no one ever seems exactly sure until the last minute when it will start, especially during the rainy season where the moon can be obscured by clouds.

A vague plan for where to position things on the land was forming as we cut away the undergrowth. A motley crew consisting of myself, Tierno, the prophetic witch doctor who'd massaged me after our accident; Seikou, a Gambian "smooth jam DJ"; a couple of guys I recognised from local *djembe* groups, and my current neighbour/all round good egg, Bakary, cleared the land and built a fence around the perimeter.

Rising early before the heat, we'd hack away. I was keen to keep the good stuff and Tierno was on hand, as an African herbs man, to ensure plants and trees with medicinal value stayed. There is a tendency for locals here to chop all the trees down and extend the Sahara a few more hundred metres.

If we did that, we'd have no shade and a dust storm every time the wind blows, so I made sure that did not happen. However, there were many prickly and poisonous plants, as well as parasites that overtake and strangle the good stuff, so all that had to go.

Perhaps predictably, after a couple of hours I was drenched, covered in mosquito bites and half the skin from my right hand was ripped off. A little physical exertion and the toubab dissolved into a mess, but it felt good. After years of work in front of a computer screen, it felt exhilarating to get my hands dirty, especially as I was building a home for my new family.

We had to be mindful of snakes and other creepy crawlies. A python and a two-metre long monitor lizard were spotted – an excitement lacking in my small Brighton garden. Where parents in Europe may worry about their children playing in the road, I have to be mindful of snakes. Twitchers, take note: there are birds everywhere here and a friend told me he spotted 108 species in 10 days.

As the summer progressed, the heat and discomfort levels gradually built up, sometimes reaching close to 100 percent humidity. Any wetter and we'd be swimming. When you stepped out of the shower, you would be wet again. However, being a glass-half-full kind of a guy, I prefer to think, not that it's the rainy season but that:

It's mango time!

MANGO TIME

Khady is preparing soup. I say soup. It's a large platter of chicken, potatoes and onions with a drizzle of sauce. Exactly the same as a dish we eat seemingly day after day.

I comment on this.

"Toubab soup has too much water and is only fit for bandits," she tells me.

"But this is the same as all the other meals," I say.

"Yes, but you like soup."

For breakfast, for snacks and after each soup dinner, Khady peels and slices mangoes. This more than compensates for the sameness of our other dishes. I eat so much of this fruit that instead of Chérif Mané, I have become known as Chérif Mango. Every other tree in Abene is seemingly a mango tree and they drip from the trees throughout the rains. Trucks pour in from Dakar, buying them by the tonne, but there're still enough to overdose on and many go to waste. These mangoes aren't like the hard lumps that we pay a fortune for in England. No, they're soft, sensuous, with flavour that explodes in your mouth as if you've swallowed an entire packet of Opal Fruits[6].

Whilst I hacked and chopped at the undergrowth on our plot of land, Khady took control of the new trees we wanted to plant before the main rains started, so that they'd flourish and grow quickly in the warm, wet air. We planted mango, orange, lemon, guava, cashew and banana trees. This felt like a good start.

One of the joys of living in a tropical paradise is the fruit, and the anticipation of your favourite coming into season. I eat more fruit than ever here, much of which I've never even seen before. In the winter, I enjoy freshly squeezed orange juice every morning. Bananas come in many varieties all year round: small, large, green, yellow and red. In the spring, it's the cashew fruit (it took me a while to work out what this fruit was). Cashews do literally grow on trees round here and when they ripen, if you can beat the chickens when they fall from the tree, there's a delicious fruit with a nut on the top by the stem. Although I like the taste, they do suck all the moisture from your mouth and are more palatable when crushed to make juice. Roasting the nuts on the fire and then everyone sitting around shelling and eating them is another simple pleasure.

[6]Very sweet, tangy candies that were common in England in the 1970s and '80s. In the United States, they go by the name of Starburst.

After the rains, locals eat *dita*, or as I've christened them, *oeuf vert* (green eggs). Beneath a thin brittle shell lies a thin layer of bright green powdery fruit around a stone. Again, much nicer as a juice as there's way too much work involved for too little reward, in my opinion, although the Senegalese disagree. My favourite is probably jackfruit, a large spiky green fruit full of yellow chewy bubble-gum flavoured chunks. Other recent discoveries include *kouelak* (toffee-flavoured sludgy balls of fun), and a variety of young coconut from the raffia palm that yields a chewy, creamy lychee-like fruit.

As we tidied the land, secured the perimeter and hacked away the bush, the land revealed itself inch by inch. Although I'd known it was a lovely place, I quickly realised it was stunning. There were cool forest glades and a stretch of dark forest seemingly impenetrable with twisted vines and gnarly roots. I was in my element and every day I discovered my new favourite place. I uncovered a huge termite mound near the entrance which provides, to my eyes, an idyllic view as you enter our gates – like a huge orange rocket rising out of the lime-green jungle.

A natural clearing in the centre of the land revealed itself as the obvious place to build the main house. Its verandah would face a lovely stretch of forest, all within our boundaries so there would be no chance of a new development popping up and spoiling the view.

Alongside the well, the other important job was to make a fence. Parts of the land were trails that local people used as short cuts, depositing their litter along the way and we didn't want that. Along with the fruit trees, it was paramount that we kept the cows and goats off the land that would view our hard work as lunch. As we were trying to keep things as natural and African as possible, I went for a traditional wooden stake fence, with dead palm leaves to fill in the gaps.

I hired Tierno the marabout and a couple of others to build the fence and do some clearing and we agreed that this was about a week's work. I checked the going rate for materials and labour so that when we negotiated I'd have a fair idea. As usual, they asked me how much I had, rather than giving me a quote. So I gave a price based on my knowledge. They agreed and we carried on with the work. Everyone was happy.

After a few days, when the work was half completed, they asked me when I was going to buy the fencing materials. This cost was the bulk of the amount I'd already given them to make the purchase, so this came as a surprise. Khady started talking furiously and fighting my corner. They said they'd expected me to buy the materials, even though we'd blatantly agreed that the original cost covered that.

Another lesson learnt – I know this one already and should have known better, but get things in writing. I hadn't thought it was necessary as Tierno was a family member and besides, he can barely read.

We re-agreed a fair amount for the labour and then they told me the material costs, which was way cheaper than I'd expected. Incredibly, the total for all the work was now almost half of the original price. I confirmed and reconfirmed that they were happy. They were, and so was I.

They say you should never work with animals or children. I would add family. Tierno had by this point moved to Abene with his family. His wife, Fatou, was the older sister of Khady and they had three daughters, Myamoona (5), Binta (3) and Roogi (6 months). Fatou was one of the family members who came to help Khady after Gulliver's birth, even though Roogi was only three months old herself at that point. I got on really well with Fatou and we always laughed, joked and play-fought. The kids climbed all over me and loved being swung around.

After a few weeks, having a new baby and a new puppy that constantly yapped at my heels, it did become a bit too much for someone used to a quiet life, but I couldn't complain with the help they brought. I was realising that Tierno was a difficult character and the family lived a nomadic lifestyle, never staying anywhere for more than a few months. It seemed they'd stay until Tierno had upset too many people and burnt too many bridges, then they'd move. But I didn't know any of this at the time.

After helping us with Gulliver, they found a room in Abene and moved in. There would be periods when they'd visit us every day until they could see I was fed up. A week with no sightings would go by and then they'd resume. When we started on the land, Fatou would cook every day for the workers and Tierno led the team effort for clearing and building the fence.

This was all great until he started playing up, threatening others working with us, saying he was a great shaman and could cast spells to kill people. It turned out he didn't do a great job on the fence and we ended up redoing it several months later. Every time there was a small communication error he flew off the handle and acted as if I was out to cheat him. I must be one of the mellowest laid-back guys around, who always tries to sort out problems quickly and fairly. I wondered why he couldn't use his shamanic skills to judge my character.

Unfortunately, it was Khady who had to bear the brunt of the problems. Even his wife, Fatou, was often in tears, ashamed at his behaviour. There is one thing that scares a witch doctor, even one that can mystically kill people. The Mother-in-Law. When Khady's mum arrived he looked physically frightened and when he finished the work we agreed to let him go. There are plenty of good workers around and we didn't need such drama.

Meanwhile, we were still working on the never-ending fence. I'm not entirely sure how long it took the Chinese to build the Great Wall, but I suspect it was considerably quicker than ours, which seemed to take forever. What's the rush, you may think? Well, try spending months hauling water from a ten-metre deep well, dragging it a hundred metres under a blazing sun every day to water trees and then watch local goats casually saunter in and munch the fruit. That was the rush.

The first job was to install posts, called *kembo*. This is the name of the tree and its wood is very hard, immune to termites and should last my lifetime at least. One day before breakfast, I went with Tierno to a nearby village to fetch the *kembo*, which was in a mangrove swamp. We could only get Kermit so far, then had to walk back and forth with logs on our shoulders for a few hundred metres, roping in to help a group of small boys who were catching frogs.

After this, Tierno disappeared into the forest for a day, returning to say he'd found some dead trees and chopped his own *kembo* for us. We took Kermit to pick it up, and as we were dragging the logs onto the roof, a man appeared, bare foot, dressed in just a pair of shorts and swinging a large machete. He wasn't happy; it was his land and it's polite to ask. I don't like angry Africans with machetes. We sorted it out, but it was a further example of the witch doctor causing a problem. As I say, we sorted it out, but Tierno wouldn't leave it there and went round stirring up trouble that evening. Then he arrived back at my land and planted 10 cashew trees, flowers and some mandarin on my land, making it hard for me to be too angry.

After we'd dealt with the man and loaded the *kembo* onto Kermit, we returned through thick forest. I was concerned about my tyres, as I hadn't repaired my spare. The witch doctor ran ahead, like Presidential security, as I drove in first gear. He checked the floor and slashed at branches with his machete, thus we made it out in one piece.

After the *kembo* wars, we had to find palm leaves for the fence. The *kembo* provides the backbone and the palms the filling to block the gaps. Seikou and Bakary spent a morning climbing palm trees and hacking off the dead leaves, from a person's land who wanted them trimming and tidied. Then, with Kermit, we drove down forest tracks, through scary steaming swamps and into the forest, where there was a particularly intimidating pile which we managed by making several trips.

Abene is less than 10 miles from the border with the Gambia and it's a much closer option for buying materials than Ziguinchor, not to mention cheaper. I needed to buy cement to make bricks for the well. It was spitting with rain as we left home and by the time we arrived in Brikama, a large trading town that is normally hot and dusty, it was a waterlogged mud pit complete with raw sewage, after a torrential downpour. I was with Khady and Gulliver. Luckily, Kermit is an amphibian and negotiated the water-logged potholes with ease. I was sweating slightly when we were less than half way across one and the red muddy water reached the bonnet of the car. Thankfully that was the deepest point, otherwise I might still be there.

We bought the cement and negotiated transport to get it back to Abene. Apart from the fact I'd rather not have 1.5 tonnes of dusty cement in the back of Kermit, it could cause me a problem at Customs, especially as a toubab, although normally they turn a blind eye to the battered Land Rover Defenders that ply the back routes of the jungle most days. Somebody suggested I could make a good living doing this with Kermit. I'd never before considered smuggling as a career, but it's always good to have something to fall back on.

We went to a greasy spoon for lunch. It was hot outside and positively stifling after we'd entered through grimy curtains and sat at a plastic table that had broken in half and been stitched back together. As I chewed on greasy rice and an old bit of goat, I inspected the walls; these were full of tributes to Gaddafi and British footballers. I went to another shop to buy a coke from a thoroughly miserable-looking Mauritanian. As I left I noticed the display of Osama Bin Laden stickers and posters. This wasn't long after Bin Laden's death. Maybe the shopkeeper thought I was an American?

Our final job of the day was to discuss a car sales business I was thinking about, selling from the Gambia to Guinea Bissau, with the help of a Gambian mate who's spent years in England. I was surprised when I'd asked him where he'd lived.

"Glastonbury. I like to be near the hippies." He laughed at my surprise and confirmed there aren't too many Africans in deepest Somerset. He introduced me to his friend, Blackie.

I felt like I was in a 1970s sit-com as I chatted to Blackie, a middle-aged guy wearing a string vest and sporting a magnificent Afro. When asked where I was from, I told him.

"Ah, my colonial master," he exclaimed.

I apologised, thinking of the decades of oppression.

"It doesn't matter," he said. "You bring us Beckham!"

Khady, Gulliver and I took a couple of days off in the Gambia to relax. Our hotel was full of Gambian women who were smoking. According to Khady this was a sure sign that they were prostitutes, so I was instructed not to forget to wear my gris-gris, thus protecting me from any spells the women might cast.

One morning, I arrived at a café around 7am for some *breggae* (an English breakfast) on a sandy side street with a sound system pumping out reggae tunes. I saw a couple of drunk, toothless prostitutes dancing with a portly old English man. It looked like they were still partying from the night before, the ugly side of the Gambia, which is sadly all too common. I chatted to a guy from Manchester, perhaps the first I'd met not wearing an anorak. He was covered in prison tattoos and was drunk by 8am. He said he was off to Burkino Faso with a local woman who had a moonshine distillery. Then an old chubby Brit with a beer gut, tats and a string vest walked past, arm in arm between two tall, mini-skirted beauties. "Every Gambian girl's dream," I mused.

Sex tourism is rife in the Gambia and to a lesser extent in the beach resorts of the Casamance. Unlike Thailand or other Asian countries, where typically you see older men with young Asian girls, here, mature European women can easily find an eager, fit young man with a grin and a six pack to satisfy their holiday needs.

For me, Gambia is a place where I can get my fill of pizza, Indian, Chinese or other "toubab" foods, although that often comes at a price. On this occasion I traced the dodgy stomach to a Nigerian chop shack. The food was probably fine as it bubbles all day in a cauldron on the fire, but the dishes and cutlery left much to be desired. I'd not had stomach problems for years. Tap water, salad, dodgy chop shacks – all fair game when Fenton's hungry or thirsty. After four years in Vietnam and more elsewhere in the world, my digestive system is pretty robust. But on this occasion my defences were broken and I spent the evening dry heaving and on the toilet.

If you have ever been to an outdoor music festival you may think you have experienced toilet hell, but believe me, compared to some places in Africa, these are perfumed palaces. When I read back through my travel diaries, I find that I have spent more time discussing the state of the toilets and arduous journeys than the local sights. After all, everyone knows what the Taj Mahal looks like, but rereading about doing the Kathmandu quick step with a belly full of Delhi takes me straight back to the subcontinent.

I've experienced a psychedelic whirlpool of maggots in Malawi, approached rooms from which even the slugs are fleeing in China, holes in India that looked like they'd simply cut out the middle man and in Timbuktu, it looked like a camel had gotten there before me. Once in Goa, I entered a palm leaf cubicle only to be faced with clean bare earth without even a hole. I was momentarily confused until I heard grunting. A pig's snout hungrily snuffled its way under the wall – almost negating the need for toilet paper. The infamous toilet pig produces a particularly succulent meat, although I personally avoid bacon sandwiches when I know these old-school appliances are near.

Before leaving the Gambia, we had one more run-in with officialdom.

"Hello, how are you?" I said cheerfully, attempting to charm the Customs chap.

"We're managing," came the reply. He demanded my car papers.

"Yes, your papers are in order which is very, very good."

But ...

"And you are an Englishman. Good people."

Just say what you mean.

"We are the same, you and me."

Yeah, yeah, I know, black and white, we're all the same, nice to be nice, one love, one heart, let's rip the toubab off one more time ...

"If I told you that you are a driver and I am a Customs man, you would know we think alike."

Here it comes ...

"So, do you have a little something for me?"

There, it didn't hurt. Just spit it out and save us all

some time. As he was a shiny happy person, I gave him a packet of green tea from my emergency "checkpoint stash".

One of the problems of building in this part of Senegal is money. Not so much the matter of having it, but getting enough and transporting it. Our nearest bank machine is around 50 miles away. There's no bank at all in Abene and just a simple credit mutual in nearby Kafountine, which accepts Western Union transfers if you're prepared to accept the high charges. At this point, I didn't have a local account and was drawing cash directly from my UK account with a Visa card with a daily maximum of £300. That's fine for general living but not when building. Costs are far cheaper than in Europe, but not that cheap.

I also felt the need to get away periodically. It's the traveller in me – I can't stay in one place for too long, no matter how idyllic. Although I have a few trip ideas up my sleeve, whilst building, trips to the provincial capital, Ziguinchor, about 70 miles away, and the Gambia are about all I can manage.

I always found the name Ziguinchor (pronounced zig-in-shore) a bit odd, unlike any other local place name, but recently discovered its meaning. It's based on an old Portuguese phrase: *Cheguei e choram*, "I came and they cry," referring to the slave trade. The Portuguese established

Ziguinchor as a trading post in 1645. They referred to the inhabitants at the time as Falupos, which translates as "swamp people" and the Diola consider themselves to be their successors.

Before purchasing my car Kermit, my trips consisted of hours of waiting in *gare routières* (bus and taxi stations), interspersed by a bit of actual travelling. I'm not grumbling, though. In fact I find *gare routières* to be absolutely fascinating, especially in a large town like Ziguinchor.

I would usually turn up sometime before the sun rises for a long trip as it's cooler and I have more chance of bagging the front passenger seat which has some leg room. Otherwise, I'd be stuck in the third row – what would normally be a car boot, where they put a seat for three more people. Once I have my place, it's a waiting game. Prices are set by the government and profit margins are non-existent so drivers are forced to cram in as many people and as much luggage as possible to ensure they make a few pennies.

I'll usually grab myself a couple of café *toubas*. I'm still not entirely sure what gives this local coffee its distinctive liquorice-like taste, but it's good, if a little too sweet. There's invariable a stall on wheels, where the boy will scoop the coffee from a cauldron and then pour it back and forth between two cups, sometimes reaching impressive heights, and building up a cappuccino froth.

Then there are the urchins. Little ragged boys called the Talibe, often barefoot, faces covered in dust and snot, often wearing a Unicef or a Barack Obama "Time for Change"

T-shirt. Groups of them, carrying old tomato puree tins, walk around chanting for spare change. Tragically, they are controlled by gang leaders who will beat them if they don't reach their quota. One modern-day Fagin was charged recently for beating a boy to death. Years of working with homeless people has led me to believe it's best to give money to an organisation rather than to an individual, but in this case it's hard to resist.

Market stalls sell just about everything, as long as it's cheap and Chinese. Women sell *bissap*, a Ribena-like drink in little plastic bags made from hibiscus. Mangoes are sold from large enamel bowls carried in on their heads. A more modern phenomenon is men selling mobile phone top up cards – the future is very much Orange in West Africa. Small stalls with dubious hygiene make omelettes and stick them in rolls with brown lumpy mayonnaise stored in buckets and not refrigerated. Often there's a choice of a spaghetti roll or a macaroni roll, so it's lucky I'm not on the Atkins diet.

Baye Fall boys with their large turbans, masses of beads and long robes, collect for charity. Goats wander round hoovering up the discarded mango skins and other rubbish. There's a motley collection of bush taxis, buses, trucks and abandoned vehicles which are in a really bad way. On top of all of this are the mad men, the hucksters, the Liberian refugees looking for an English speaker, the baggage handlers and the mass of people all seemingly moving all of their worldly possessions.

Where I once thought nothing of riding on the roof of a rickety bus with a one-mile drop to the side, I must have lost my nerve as I now really struggle with public transport. That was the impetus behind me buying the Land Rover. I guess that wasn't surprising after the bus crash. Following that, the next bush taxi I took hit a goat. Not long after, I hired a guide with a motorbike, got on the back and only then discovered he had no idea how to drive it. He revved wildly and we took off on the back wheel, me screaming, before crashing 100 metres or so down the gravel track. I took all the skin off one knee and one elbow. I was wearing the gris-gris and maybe it brought me luck again as we were within a few metres of a medical clinic.

We finally left for Ziguinchor in the "*sept place*" (seven places) bush taxi. It's thrilling to hurtle down the red mud road as the great orange sun rises above the forests, blue skies above, vivid green forest to the side and children running alongside shouting "toubab". More often, it's like sitting in a sauna, fully clothed in an uncomfortable squashed position whilst someone throws dust over you. After a long drive across a rutted road crossing a mangrove swamp, we crossed a long bridge across the river into the city. On this occasion, a perfect rainbow formed, the ends touching down on either side of the river. I was amazed to see dolphins swimming in the waters and watched as one jumped out of the water into the arch of the rainbow. Well, that beats the typical wildlife image in my hometown of Brighton – seagulls feeding on discarded kebabs from the previous night.

I stayed at Casse Afrique, a small and friendly hotel with a cast of shady characters who could be the inspiration for a novel. There's Coley the night watchman with his Sherlock Holmes pipe; Laurent the Guinean shark fisherman whose boat was stolen by pirates from Togo; a woman who had crossed the Sahara on a space hopper, the American pilot who rescues slaves from Sudan; Terry the bandit; escaped French convicts; dubious ladies propping up the bar and bats that dive bomb you in the evening. With free Wifi (but you have to watch out for falling mangoes in the garden; one destroyed the television and narrowly missed my laptop) you can almost forgive the state of the plumbing.

I turned up and a new staff member who I didn't know greeted me, showed me to my room then asked me for 2,000 CFA to buy some tea and sugar, which he said he'd deduct from the bill. It later turned out that no one in the hotel had ever heard of him.

This time I wanted to transfer money from my Gambian account to the Ziguinchor branch. Unfortunately the transfer limit was fairly low and I had to stay three days, transferring the maximum allowance each day. Customer service in Senegal, in my experience, lags behind that of the UK. Once I'd awaited my turn in the queue, I sat as the bank teller, looking bored, shuffled endless papers, tapped absentmindedly at her keyboard whilst taking regular phone calls, seemingly to her *chérie*.

After signing something and then sitting counting flies for another 20 minutes, I enquired how long it would take.

She replied that I was free to go. So I'd been wasting my time and that of the increasingly long queue behind. To me, such inefficiency signals incompetence but here, as in many developing countries, it's a sign of power. The customer must be polite, deferential and patient or else you won't get what you need.

Once the business was over, I was free to enjoy some decent food and mooch around in the Big Smoke. I visited a French-run restaurant that had been recommended and excitedly ordered Thai green curry, breaking one of my food rules. Here's a tip: stick to foods people know, French or Senegalese in this case. I've been disappointed so many times, you'd have thought I'd have learnt by now; Indian curries in Paris; macaroni cheese in the Himalayas; English breakfast in Laos – all recipes for disaster.

The Thai curry appeared to be *maffe*, the local peanut sauce, with a little lemon-grass powder added. Edible, but hardly the fragrant fusion of spices and coconut milk that I'd been hoping for. I'd just finished when I was approached by a woman I knew. It was Binta, who owns a shop in Abene. She asked to join me, which was fine; it's good to speak a little English with someone occasionally. Then she asked if she could see my hotel. I'm starting to think I might be a little naïve, as I said sure, thinking maybe we'd have a coke and a chat.

We got back to the hotel where she asked for a little "jiggy jiggy boom boom". There then followed a five-minute struggle. I ended up apologising and telling her that of course she's a lovely, beautiful woman, but I don't just "jiggy jiggy boom boom" with anyone I meet over a Thai curry. She then pulled out various radios and mobile phones: if she couldn't have me, perhaps she could sell me something.

I'll often go to the Perroquet, a decent French-run hotel on the banks of the river Casamance, to use the internet and work on my website. The bar offers a fresh breeze, shade, cold drinks and views across the mile-wide river over to mangrove swamps and fishermen pottering about in brightly coloured *pirogues*. This may well be the most picturesque office I've had the pleasure to work in.

That evening I got chatting to a girl from Basque country. Zurina was keen to check out the nightlife, so we headed to the Bombolon, a dingy club just down the road. Senegalese nightclubs are curious places. The DJ sat in a booth playing tunes from a laptop. When we arrived, he was playing *mblax*, which I really like. This is a unique Senegalese pop music with furious drum rhythms and is great fun. This later merged into modern Senegalese and Nigerian pop, which I loath. There is usually an insanely catchy melody which you can't get out of your head for weeks, and the vocals are auto-tuned to robotic levels that make me want to tear off my ears and throw them into another dimension. Horrible, but everyone loves it and you can't go anywhere without someone blaring it out of their tinny mobile phone speaker.

The clubs are always very dark, with all the lights trained on the dance floor. Surrounding this are many booths where people are almost invisible and surrounding the dance floor itself are huge mirrors. Ladies with no apparent sense of embarrassment stand in front and perform their moves. The sort of thing one might do in a bedroom, perhaps with a tennis-racket guitar.

Zurina dragged a friendly group of prostitutes onto the dance floor before turning to me and beckoning. Before too long, Zurina and I were strutting our stuff and mirror dancing. The horror, the horror.

Sometimes there seemed to be periods of time, which felt like months, where nothing would go right. Occasionally it would all reach a head. Gulliver became a little sick and was awake most nights. I became feverish; everybody seems to become a bit feverish in the rainy season. Then I wanted to make a circle of logs for people to sit around the fire. They were big logs, so I tied them to the back of Kermit and dragged them across the land. As I drove over a spiky tree stump, I heard a hiss and felt that familiar sinking feeling as two brand-new tyres were shredded.

Not long after, I collected some palm leaves for the fence while rather foolishly wearing flip flops. A thorn stuck in the back of my heel. I pulled it out and forgot about it. Big mistake. In the tropics you should clean and put antiseptic cream on even the most trivial of cuts.

A few days later, I awoke with a hot, throbbing foot. I couldn't sleep afterwards and when I stood on it the next morning, a jet of pain shot up my leg and a plug of hot pus squirted out the back of my heel. I was put on penicillin and laid with my leg up for the next few days. The roads leading to surrounding villages were washed away in this period so travelling became difficult and we spent weeks on end watching the never-ending rain from our verandah.

It wasn't just me that was afflicted. My very practical Basque friend, Tasta, called me one day telling me he'd gotten bogged down in the mangrove swamp in his jeep. Could I pull him out? There ensued a Laurel and Hardy type farce, where Kermit also sank. Then the truck that came to pull us both out sank. We were going round in circles, one becoming free, pulling another out and getting stuck again. That's life in the rainy season.

The fence was finally nearing completion, although I soon learnt that like Scotland's Forth Bridge, it would never be truly finished. I felt sufficiently confident to start planting some fruit trees that would now be safe-guarded from the goats. I had another spurt of planting fruit trees; yet more mandarin and orange, mango, banana, coconut, avocado and guava. Also many flowers, bamboo and aloe vera. Khady planted *manioc*, a delicious root vegetable eaten across Africa, as well as corn, peanuts, beans and sweet potatoes. The next day, squirrels had eaten all of the corn, so I made a scarecrow. We also hung up some old Nollywood DVDs that I couldn't bring myself to watch, as well as a couple of bits of metal that clatter in the wind[7]. Hopefully, one or more of these would be effective.

We were keen to get started on our first house as we were "commuting" to work from the rented place nearby. A quote from a local builder came in at maybe five or six times the regular price, so I chuckled and when he asked if I'd give him the job, replied "*Inshallah*". This is a great word for saying yes to something when you don't mean it. It'll be up to the will of Allah.

Khady was fairly sure that Tierno told this guy to drive the price up so he could take a commission. We're not certain, but it wouldn't surprise me. Tierno was approaching the end of his contracted jobs and then he was out. I think he knew it so was delaying, to ride the gravy train as long as possible. Luckily for me, Khady fights my corner. She's unique amongst local girls in being a very strong, outspoken woman with a crazy sense of humour and who speaks directly and puts people straight if she thinks they're talking "the blah blah thing" as she puts it.

One day, her friend came round and asked if I'd buy her a phone. Khady immediately jumped in and said, "yes, go on Simon, go to your money tree". Then she turned to her friend and asked if she'd like me to buy her a car and a house as well.

Although my local language skills are limited, I generally have a vague idea of what's being said. If it isn't an extended

---

[7]Nollywood is the name given to the popular Nigerian film industry. In my opinion, the discs are more suited for scaring birds than viewing.

Khady Mane

Bass, who first invited me to Abene,
with my Land Rover Kermit reflected in his shades

Stilt dancers take a break on Kermit

Essamaye, a devil dancer

Three *Koumpos*

Simba the Lion Man

Gulliver with his cousins
l-r: Roogi, Myamoona, Gulliver, Binta

The original Little Baobab (tree)
in front of our first house

Home sweet home

Gulliver and our house

The Casamance – a typical landscape

Tony, the blind and deaf traveller,
relaxing in an Abene beach bar

Drinking *bounok* – palm wine

Khady dances at Abene Festivalo

Life is beautiful

Walking home, Abene beach

greeting it's usually about money. Apart from staple items, there's rarely a fixed price, which results in constant arguments, quibbling and jealousy.

"If there was no such thing as money, we'd all be a lot happier," remarked Khady and I'm often inclined to agree. Did you know that only 11 percent of the money in America actually exists? The rest is electronic. That fried my brain a little.

Abene is a small rural village with many musicians and artists. It doesn't attract people seeking five-star luxury or package-tourist type destinations. Most toubabs here are regular folk seeking "the real Africa" and most toubabs living here have a similar story to mine. They were recommended Abene, visited for a few days and fell in love with the village – and often with a person – and so they came back.

The average daily wage here is around £1 to £2 per day and many people will have periods with no work at all. So, for example, a backpacker who's travelling for a couple of weeks on say £10 per day is by comparison a rich person. If I told somebody it was possible to earn £100 or more a day in England, they'd be absolutely incredulous. Although I'd try to explain the cost of rent or a mortgage, of food, petrol and everything else, it wouldn't matter. That was a prince's sum.

The issue that always seems to be a problem between Western and more traditional societies is giving money to the family. Here, if an African has money he spreads it around, giving to friends, parents, brothers, sisters and so on. Although I admire the system, many people are taken advantage of and I've seen local people on meagre wages giving everything to their families, when other brothers are living in Europe and contributing nothing. Trying to make some money to save and build a business is near-impossible for many as any spare cash goes back to the family or to marabouts. Invariably, when you see a successful African venture, there's a family member in Europe or a toubab behind it.

It's sometimes awkward for me. I have enough money for my lifestyle and for my plans, but only if I manage it carefully. This is the great cultural difference. Most local people subsist from day to day and don't have the opportunity to save, budget and make plans.

Very often I visit people and they will demand money for nothing. I will open my first-aid kit for local people, give free rides, employ people and pay fair prices for services and there are certain projects I'd like to support when I have the means, but I don't want to support a culture of hand-outs and dependency when the reality is we don't have serious poverty in this village compared to other parts of Africa and everybody eats.

Khady and I have found our own solution for living in financial harmony. I've helped her set up two small businesses – a motorbike taxi service and selling fish, so she now earns her own money. She's happy and proud to be making a contribution without constantly asking me for financial help. My incomes pay for the larger costs; the land, the house build, the car and holidays. A partnership between the third and first worlds may not be financially equal, but we've found a balance that we're happy with.

The work on our many projects had slowed due to heavy rains and problems finding the few remaining *kembo* that were required for the fence. One of the well diggers was no longer well. He had an infected hand, which he was urinating upon every day, a local method of curing it. After several weeks of digging and lifting the sand out, one bucket at a time, the diggers finally struck water and the well was under way.

Around this time we started work on the small house. With the rains and hardships, time seemed to drag indefinitely, but a glance at my diaries shows that I signed the land ownership papers on 22 June, started the house build on 24 July and we'd moved in the first week of September, so we didn't do too badly.

The foreman was Yancoba, another of Khady's uncles. He worked with three young guys, all part of the extended family. I was taking a bit of a chance here. Whilst we were getting family rates and it's a good way for me to support the family, the downside is that things can get awkward if problems occur. Khady assured me there wouldn't be any problems and on this occasion, with the builders at least, she was right.

I had to send money for the builders to travel to Abene, which is the normal procedure. For example, if I want the police to sort out a problem, I have to give some petrol money to them to get here, as they have nothing. Despite my many complaints, there are some good African systems in place; in this case I just gave the cash to a local shop which somehow sent it by text message to a shop in Bignona, where Yankoba picked it up.

It wasn't until Yankoba arrived that I discovered that he was blind. Not only that, but after I sent the money, I was expecting him the next day. That day came and went, as did the next. Khady called him and then cheerfully told me the reason.

"Don't worry, they'll be here tomorrow. Their house just fell down, so they have to build an emergency new place. That's why they're late."

I wasn't quite sure whether to be worried that my newly hired (blind) builder's house that he had personally constructed had fallen down or to be impressed that he could rebuild it in just two days. To be honest, by this time these things were beginning to roll off me. I laughed and figured it would all turn out all right. One day. Maybe.

Many houses were washing away this year and I later learnt I was living through the heaviest rains in 40 years. Traditionally, houses are built with *banku* (mud blocks made with the sand from termite mounds), but also traditionally they collapse in the rainy season. With the current rains there was a good chance that a house constructed solely of *banku* would collapse, like Yankoba's had. So we decided to mix *banku* with some cement. This is Africa and as I was learning, if something could go wrong, the chances are it would.

Finally Yancoba and the builders arrived to start making the blocks, using a brick press. This was a manual contraption, where one spaded the *banku* and cement mixture into a mould, a metal plate was placed on top and then one of the guys levered this down using all his weight to compact the mixture.

The brick was then carefully placed in the sun to harden. Except it was rainy season, so we had to run and cover them with plastic sheets every time the heavens opened. The other builders included Diannah, a quiet chap who wore spectacles. If you saw him in Europe, you might presume he was an accountant or a businessman. Although a slim, unassuming-looking guy, when he took his shirt off he looked like the Terminator.

Oeuff was a young guy who kept falling in love. First with Khady's friend Nanky, which prompted me to ask if he was having hanky panky with Nanky. Later on with Oumey, a young local girl. He proposed to her within a week but alas, she spurned him. Oeuff (French for egg) was a nickname. An abbreviation of his full name, Erfokken, so I guess it could have been worse. The third builder was Vieux, who I nicknamed "VIEUX!" as he couldn't say anything without yelping it like James Brown.

These guys would not only build this house, but would return the following year to build the main one, so we'd end up spending several months in their company; it's normal here to host and feed workmen while you're employing them.

The foundations were dug and they started on the walls. I employed the "kick test", a trick I invented in Vietnam while building a farm. People would try to reduce the amount of cement used in construction so they could steal the leftovers. If walls fell over when I kicked them, they weren't good enough. In this case, the guys weren't stealing cement but were so used to building to the absolute cheapest standards that they'd consistently reduce the required amounts out of a false sense of economy.

Tierno had by this point disappeared whilst his wife Fatou and the three little ones, had been visiting daily. Fatou was obviously worried sick and didn't know if he'd return. I played a lot with the children, something their father never did and which I mostly enjoyed but they were very demanding. As a toubab I'm an object of curiosity to kids, but local Dads, in my experience, seem to be stand-offish and stern. It's not unusual to find me walking along with four or five little rascals hanging off of me.

Then there was Maimoona, a bright 12-year-old girl from next door whose mother died and her father remarried. The new mother didn't feed her, so she preferred spending time with us rather than at home. She generally arrived before we awoke, swept the yard and then spent the day helping Khady cook, clean, wash and scrub – when not at school –

in exchange for meals, pocket money and a family environment. She was a good cook, but tended to overuse the stock cubes beloved by everyone in Senegal, so I nicknamed her after them: "Jumbo".

I like food to be properly seasoned, but jumbo is a hideously salty chemical creation that makes everything taste the same. I've been campaigning to ban it in our kitchen, with limited success. A year or two later, we unofficially adopted Jumbo when her father's second spouse left. Khady told me she'd probably be raped at home by local boys, as she'd be there alone much of the time. I'm not sure if that's true, but no matter: she's a bright, friendly girl who enjoys playing with Gulliver, helping Khady and swimming in the sea with me. So now Jumbo is a little baobab.

As we collected materials to build the roof, I had flashbacks to the Harrison Ford movie, *The Mosquito Coast*. In the film, he drags his family into the jungles of central America to build an ice factory. There are scenes of howling monsoons with rains and high winds lashing as Ford fights to hold it together.

I'd taken Kermit along with Jumbo's father, Bakary, to pick up joists to support the thatched roof. We drove deep into the jungle, and not for the first time, I vowed this was the last time I'd take such dire routes. Bakary had spent the last couple of days cutting the struts from the strong palm trunks that everyone uses here, as they're immune from the termites and last for years. There were 60 struts, which was two loads. The heavens opened during the first load. It was about 6pm and we needed to finish, otherwise, someone else might have found and taken them.

Within a couple of minutes we were soaked to the skin and steaming after a long and irresponsibly hot day. We continued loading as lightening flashed and thunder rumbled. Then we drove back, first off-road through thick palms and ferns and then onto a track of sorts, through potholes where water reached the bonnet of Kermit. Some struts were knocked off the roof by overhead branches. Already soaked to the skin, we waded through the mud and gloom, reaching down and reloading. After dumping the first batch, we went back for more. By now it was dark and our work lit only by the lightening.

One of my life long dreams has been to live in a thatched cottage. I was however, envisioning perhaps a 400-year-old place in deepest Somerset, not a round mud hut in West Africa. I make it sound worse than the reality. It's a perfectly lovely round mud hut that may not last 400 years but should see me out. A carpenter constructed the palm struts and then Bakary thatched it with bundles of straw, cut from the edges of nearby mangrove swamps. After torrential downpours I slightly nervously went back to inspect and the inside was as dry as a bone.

All that was left was to dig the soak-away toilet pit and connect this to the bathroom, install the wiring, connect to solar panels, finish the floor and fix the doors, windows and mosquito screens. First house built. Done!

I attached the solar panel to the roof and connected it to the batteries and inverter, which converts the battery power to mains power. It was an exciting moment for me to flick the switch. And then there was light! It was necessary for one of us (me) to move in swiftly for security's sake. The house was nearly ready and we just needed to fit the doors and windows.

Quite frankly, I was excited to sleep in a room with ventilation. Normally I swelter in a hot room where we can't open the window because of the "spirits". As I arrived with my torch, book and a token machete to keep everyone happy, I noticed the workers had rigged up plastic covers on the windows and one builder told me he would stay and sleep with me for protection. I appreciated the fact that they were trying to look after me but after much pleading I told them I was perfectly capable of surviving a night alone. I thanked them for the plastic windows, then ripped them down as soon as they left.

Silence.

I paraded around whistling "zippity-doo-dah" and thinking back over the past couple of months. We had done remarkably well to complete everything in such a short space of time, and in the rains. There was still a long way to go, but at least we had a comfortable house on our own property and could slow down for a while before beginning the main house.

I'd learnt a lot and made some mistakes during the build, but that was okay, it is how you learn.

I'd been open to possibility as many had passed up on the land due to it being so overgrown. Once cleared and tidied, everybody agrees it is a place of beauty.

I'd stayed true to my vision of natural designs despite pressure to go for easier options.

I'd taken my time and not been rushed into bad decisions.

I'd learnt never to pay for work until it was completed.

I was sensitive to local traditions, whether I believed them or not. Khady's much happier knowing the land has been blessed by a marabout and that we have buried a goat's horn or two.

I no longer have any expectations of anything going to plan and there are always "those days".

I will never again begin a project at the start of the monsoon.

Finally, I will always check my land for spiky tree stumps before driving across it.

I was excited about our new life at the Little Baobab, but first we had to deal with a tragedy. Khady's father came to see us and it was clear he didn't have long to live.

THE SOUL
OF AFRICA

We are at the house of a marabout with Khady's father.
A last-ditch attempt to find out what is wrong. Khady
tells me he has "frogs in his water". After listening to the
symptoms, the marabout brews up a tea-like drink and
with a grimace, her father drinks it down.

It works fast. He whips down his trousers and starts
pissing blood. A thick worm-like creature, 10 cm long,
appears from his penis. The creature is dead, and pops
out onto the floor with much blood, her father cringing
in agony. The smell of iron fills the room. Khady's father
chirps up and seems a different man. He is told to take
the tea again in a few days and that basically he should
now be fine.

Bang, bang! "Simon, Simon ..."

It was pitch black. I was sleeping alone in our new
house. I'd been there a week and unfortunately it was not as
comfortable as I had imagined as the cement was not yet dry;
I was constantly damp and mould was growing on my arms.

The banging continued. "Who's there?" I croaked, feeling
knackered as I'd been up until 2am swatting insects.

"Khady."

I opened the shutter. She was standing with an umbrella, the wind howling and torrential rains soaking her. The palm tree behind was bent double with the howling gale.

"What time is it?"

"4am," she replied. "My father, help me."

Khady's Dad had been staying with us for a couple of weeks. I'd offered to take him to the hospital but he refused, saying they'd perform an operation that would kill him. But we knew that if he didn't go he would die. We'd reached a stalemate.

Khady had nursed him, but still it looked like the end was near. He was almost unconscious and we needed to get to hospital. I pulled on some clothes and climbed through the window (the door-frame cement was still setting) and landed in a muddy puddle, up to my thighs. We jumped into Kermit and I started a three-point turn, leaving the main track. I felt the whole vehicle sink, shifted into four-wheel drive, but to no avail – we were sinking into quicksand. I climbed out to see that the wheels had disappeared and we'd be going nowhere.

Khady found another driver, but her father refused to go. He knew that he was dying and didn't want to put anyone to any trouble. He wanted to see the local marabout instead. Later, having dug Kermit from the swamp, using many logs and two jacks, we visited the marabout where he'd urinated the snake. We crossed our fingers.

In spite of the marabout's efforts, two days later he died. We had to confirm that he was definitely dead, and I did the deed. I didn't think about it too much at the time, but that's quite a responsibility. As a former lifeguard, I can check a pulse and whether someone's breathing and think (hope) I got it right. The funeral would be that day which is typical in traditional cultures without refrigeration. We borrowed the village coffin (the body is transported in this and then removed for burial) and prepared to take him back to Khady's mother in their home village for the funeral and burial.

It was a hellish drive, taking more than two hours to cover 20 miles. We got bogged down in pothole after pothole but were in a convoy with another Land Rover and helped each other, literally pushing and dragging the cars through the swamp. I arrived in the remote village exhausted. The house was full with the entire village and people from across the province. Alfouseynou Mané was a much loved and respected man. Although I didn't know him very well, the biggest tribute I can pay is that Khady is one of the wisest, most honest, direct and straight-talking people that I've met in Africa. She tells me that this is due to her father.

Funerals here are a little different. Everyone arrives and takes over the house and usually some of the neighbouring houses. People sit on mats on the floor for much of the day, quietly reflecting. Compared to the conveyor belt system of the West, I find this quite therapeutic. How often do we sit and meditate for an entire day on just one person?

At the Dad's funeral, the men took off in a procession, carrying the coffin. As we left, many women broke down, wailing and screaming. We took the coffin into a beautiful jungle glade surrounded by giant ferns and baobab trees. His body was removed, lowered into a grave dug by family members and prayers said.

Khady's aunt, the one who stopped her from attending school, was there. Khady later learnt that she pocketed all the donations people had left at the funeral, leaving her mother with nothing.

It wasn't my first funeral that year, nor the only one with mysterious circumstances. A few weeks before Gulliver was born, Khady's cousin, Vieux (not the builder) was killed on a motorbike whilst drunk, 15 minutes after offering us both a lift. Who knows if we'd have been injured or if by changing the course of events, he'd still be alive? I try not to think about those scenarios. To a Westerner, it's fairly clear that this was a drink-driving accident waiting to happen, but it's not quite that simple in Africa.

On the day of Vieux's funeral, I was told that the family claimed a phantom horse had appeared weeks earlier which had passed on the message that two family members would die. So, after Vieux died, there was a panic, everyone being cleansed with medicine provided by the marabout and protected with new gris-gris. Even I had a new one.

At the funeral, people broke down and talked in tongues. Other family members restrained them and carried them away. In Senegalese society, emotion is suppressed and I'd assumed that a funeral was one of the few chances to express complete abandon but was later told that these people were channelling the lad's voice and he was crying out that he wasn't meant to die. There were even rumours that he was trying to tell us he'd been murdered. Considering that he'd been paralytically drunk, I doubt it.

A few days later the second death occurred when Vieux's father died. He was old and bedridden, so it's not that surprising, but a little creepy, given the equine premonition, even to a cynic like me.

Whilst discussing this with his friends, I was told of people powerful enough to transport themselves to Europe, in a ghost-like fashion, to kill their enemies. My friend told me it was a sort-of vampire airport. For a moment, I had an image of Goths queuing at Heathrow, but realised it was simply the only analogy he could make with his limited English. We'd watched a couple of vampire films so that was his term for the supernatural and spirit world.

Forty days after Khady's father's death, we went back to the village for the follow-up ceremony. I found myself bouncing down a sandy track through the jungle with a one-armed bandit drinking whisky. Khady's brother, Pap Mané, was known as the Grand Bandit, a term akin to loveable rogue – and yes, he had one arm.

Family, friends and villagers had gathered at the house and as is the custom, I had to greet them all. This entails shaking hands with every man and many of the women. Younger women and girls perform a little curtsey, a tradition that seems to have disappeared back in England, unless you're meeting the Queen. Every time I go to a house, I have to shake hands with everybody. Sometimes I will arrive and think there's one or two people there, shake their hands and then notice 10 more guys sitting in the gloom and have to carry on, when I'm often just trying to get something to drink.

As usual there were dozens of ragged little urchins, all eager to climb over me and wipe their snotty hands on my clothes. I love it. It's often sad, though, as it's not uncommon for one or two to be absent. When I enquire, I'm told they've died. There's rarely a reason. I have a lovely photograph taken only a year ago, five children all doubling up with giggles. Two are now dead.

Traditionally families are large in order to ensure there are plenty of kids to work, to provide for the parents and to account for high levels of mortality. Khady told me that as parents do have five, six or more kids, they don't pay as much attention to individual children and that's one reason so many are left to fend for themselves. Somebody said to me recently they thought life was cheaper in Africa, or words to that effect, but that's not true. When there is a death, the grief of the family is real and no different to anywhere else. The mourning process is long and more drawn out with various ceremonies in the weeks, months and years after the death. Many people wear necklaces with a laminated photograph of a deceased brother or family member.

At the same time, people are closer to death than most of us in developed countries. It is far more common given poverty, nutrition and the lack of clean water, medicine and trained doctors. People will delay a visit to the hospital as they can't afford it or will rely on marabouts and traditional medicine.

Rarely a month goes by where someone connected to me here doesn't die.

Upon arrival in the family village, a buffalo was dispatched and I was handed a head-sized chunk of its flesh, wrapped in banana leaves, that had been cooked in a delicious peppery stew. I went for a stroll and many people greeted me by name as I'm one of the only toubab's to have visited this remote village, 10 miles from the nearest paved road.

Upon my first visit there, Khady took me to a *Gamou*, an Islamic gathering involving a night of praying and chanting with a Grand Marabout. He sat on a car seat inside a house, being fanned by a man in olive green robes. He was wearing a fez wrapped in a gold band and looked to me like he was trying to stay awake as followers sat, arms outstretched, palms face up before raising them to wipe their faces. In the evening, hundreds gathered to sit in plastic chairs. I waited several hours listening to endless chanting and an organ that sounded like a never-ending intro to Pink Floyd's "Shine on You Crazy Diamond". As with many African celebrations, midnight arrived and there was no sign of anything happening. I was exhausted and went to bed.

This time, we spent 24 hours sitting in the heat, greeting everyone and drinking endless cups of *attaya*. Eventually there was a big family gathering and then I was beckoned over to look though a window of the mud-brick house. I peered into the hazy gloom and saw Khady, her two sisters and two brothers sitting, legs straight ahead – all topless. The rest of the room was filled with old women, two of whom brandished green branches and were talking very fast in the Diola language. All the brothers and sisters had agonised facial expressions and were crying, except Khady – who glanced at me with a smirk on her face.

Each sibling in turn knelt on all fours and was whipped by the old women. I thought it was symbolic and gentle, but afterwards Khady had big welts across her back. She later told me this was part of the Diola cleansing process after a father has died. Over the next day or two they'd be washed in various herbal medicines. The old woman caught my eye and I was invited in. Not yet realising it was a proper whipping, I thought it sounded like fun, went in and motioned to take my shirt off.

"No, no, you're not Diola, we can't whip you."

"Oh," I said, disappointed. "In that case, can I whip someone?"

This wasn't on either; they just wanted to ask me when I was going to officially marry Khady.

I later enquired about the whipping and was told it was as a punishment for anything the father may have disapproved of or been unhappy about. In other words, Khady and I being as yet unmarried.

In little more than a year here, I'd experienced birth and death, both of which have deep animistic beliefs associated with them. In Senegal, you do not need to scratch far beneath the surface to find these beliefs in almost any area of life. This is a land of genies, spirits and spells. Almost everybody wears a gris-gris for protection.

West Africa was animistic before Islam and Christianity showed up, and as in the rest of the continent many of the traditional beliefs were absorbed and maintained within the new religions. It's not difficult to understand why the Abrahamic religions gained a foothold. Both Christianity and Islam offer Africans an afterlife, whereas traditional beliefs aren't so clear-cut, offering only the world of spirits and ancestors.

Although some Senegalese don't agree with gris-gris, they still believe they work but see them as blasphemous against God. Everyone I know wears one or more. There's a gris-gris for every occasion: to find a lover, to become pregnant, for protection against evil …

The gris-gris, sometimes known as a *juju* or fetish, is a perfect fusion of new and old: Koranic script blessed by a marabout and then tightly wrapped and sewn into a piece of leather and worn on a specific part of the body. These are worn around the waist, the neck, the upper arm or elsewhere, and offer spiritual protection.

I was once asked to wear a new gris-gris to protect me for a flight home to the UK and I've seen men work themselves into a trance and then stab and cut themselves with knives, protected by their gris-gris. The strength depends on the strength of the marabout. A Grand Marabout, a skinned black cat and a small fortune could buy you invisibility.

It's quite difficult to find information about such beliefs. Africa is very dark and there are some things I can never understand. Gris-gris are very personal and one shouldn't discuss them too much or else your enemy may prepare a counter one. The important thing for me to be mindful of is, whatever my beliefs, most Africans believe they work and, like a placebo, this belief can make them work. Witchcraft is certainly not a joke here, as you can't laugh at what you fear. People do whither away and die or fall ill when they know a spell has been cast against them, as they believe it's true and that it is going to work. I have seen some people become lethargic and change personality when they enter a house where protective gris-gris have been placed.

I've been given many gris-gris, starting of course with Ibrahima's in Dakar. The latest will protect me from knife or bullet wounds. I'm beginning to resemble a leather-bound Michelin man and wouldn't look out of place at some of Brighton's more "niche" nightclubs.

I do however like a nice gris-gris and fancied a couple of the leather pouches on a thong tied around my upper arm. I thought that if I wore them on my left arm, they'd be staring straight into the face of any police officers who tried to stop me for a bribe whilst driving. I hoped that by signifying that I'm not a tourist, the gris-gris might help.

Shortly after I made this decision, I went on a trip to the Gambia, following a route where I was previously stopped and interrogated at three different police blocks. This time, sporting a full frontal gris-gris, they all glanced at me, smiled and waved me through.

Khady once joked with me that she could go to the marabout and place a spell on me so that I'd give her all my money without complaint.

"Many toubabs have been ripped off by people here," she explained. "Why didn't they go to the police? It was because the African had marabout protection."

I suggested that maybe a toubab that hands over a large sum of money only for the receiver to disappear may realise with embarrassment how gullible he'd been and chalk it up to experience. However, if there's a choice to be made between the rational or the supernatural, the supernatural is usually chosen.

Not only humans are given gris-gris. Homes, cars and even orchards are protected. I was thinking about planting an orange grove and was discussing this with a shopkeeper friend who tells me there's big money in selling this fruit to Dakar. I enquired whether you'd lose much fruit to theft.

"No, no, you simply hang some gris-gris in the trees. Everyone knows that if they then steal the oranges their testicles will fall off."

I didn't ask what happens to female thieves. A few days later, I was walking past some tasty-looking oranges, and just as my mind turned to scrumping, I noticed gris-gris hanging from the tree. I carried on walking.

After some building problems where nothing seemed to be going right, Khady took me to Bignona. We were staying with her uncle and visiting an important marabout to be blessed, washed and provided with protection to give us a good life and a strong house. For Khady, this was something essential for her well-being as she was having nasty dreams and was worrying constantly. For me, it would be another interesting experience.

As we arrived, the massive extended family was sitting in the large house, sheltering from the rain and brewing *attaya*. A small bowl of greasy rice with a bit of onion and single leaf of cabbage had been kept to one side for us.

The house was typical, in that it's mud bricks, mud floor, well swept and with barely any possessions. People's phone numbers were scrawled on the walls with bits of charcoal. A typical kitchen will have a couple of bricks to rest pots on the fire, a few pans (made from recycled metal), a few plastic bowls for washing and a few utensils. That's about it. In fact, the Scottish explorer Mungo Parks described identical scenes, minus the plastic, during his journey across West Africa in 1795.

In the evening, one of the lads living there, Diatta, who'd helped me build my first house, wanted to take me to a local bar. Although he's a Muslim, he proudly drinks and told me something that I already knew: the Koran is contradictory about drinking alcohol and that people have only subsequently made it a rule. It's a universal trait that humans are selective about what they want to believe.

A rainy Tuesday night in Bignona is not exactly Ibiza, but I was up for a night out. We walked down a dimly lit street, dodging holes, mud and water fairly unsuccessfully, and then Diatta indicated a small hovel. We walked in to see three guys sitting hunched over their mobile phones drinking local spirits. Tables made from cheap plywood were draped with plastic tablecloths. Looking up, I saw that the ceiling was decorated with Christmas decorations. It was August.

A large old woman served us a litre of surprisingly good red wine. Although Diatta's been studying English for several years, we were able to communicate better in Diola. A chap at the next table played Christian hymns through his mobile phone and then started chatting. He wanted to speak English, but couldn't and I barely understood a word he said.

"What work do you do?" I asked.

"I'm the English teacher at the local school."

The next morning we left with Khady's uncle Yancoba and a woman friend of his. We were driving into the bush to a remote village to visit the marabout about the protective medication. There was a torrential downpour as we left the town, and then I heard the whistle of a policeman.

He demanded all my papers and got them all wet as he searched for something to try to get me on. When he realised they were in order, he made me test all my lights and indicators. Then demanded to know why I hadn't got a spanner to remove the wheel bolts. "But I have." He seemed confused. Then the woman got out, whispered something in his ear and he sheepishly waved us on. Everyone laughed and explained to me that she's a police chief from Dakar. She told him she'd report him as what he was demanding of me was not normal.

We continued towards the marabout's home, crossing a wide expanse of mangrove and then through deep forest, for mile on mile of rutted, potholed roads. His house was deep in the woods. Built from mud bricks and with a thatched roof, it blended into the surroundings. If you can imagine the gloomy interior of a medieval witch's house, you'll have a good idea of how it looked. Bunches of dried leaves, herbs and twigs hung alongside monkey skulls, like shrunken heads. Scattered around were other tools of the trade; goat horns, Arabic scrolls, dried geckos and unidentifiable body parts.

The marabout, a wise-looking old man dressed in flowing robes, was standing in the doorway. An old woman was also there and I was told she was more than 100 years old. I was surprised as she looked about 60. "Yes," said the marabout, "she only has one wrinkle and she sits on it." We sat in his bedroom as Khady discussed our needs. Then, we went outside and were presented with a bucket each of fragrant water filled with bits of wood and debris. We had to each cover our bodies in the water, then let it dip dry. Only once dry, could we repeat. We had to do this for seven cycles.

It was raining, a little chilly and the water was positively bracing. After an hour I was shivering and feeling miserable. The things I do to show solidarity to Khady and involve myself in her culture.

Then the marabout spoke, leading me to wonder if I had further case of "finding connections that are random" (probably), or "is African mysticism alive and kicking"? He told me that I would receive a job offer from a foreign country. The very same afternoon, I received a phone call from Denmark. It was my African mother, Diatou, who had been there for three months running workshops to bring African culture to schools, festivals and so on. Would I be able to go and pick her up from the airport upon her return, for which she'd pay me? Of course I would I replied, slightly disappointed if that was the job offer from abroad.

A few days later I received a visit at home from my neighbour, Kai. He dances with local group Wakily and had a favour to ask of me. They'd been invited to perform in Cote D'Ivoire and needed to put together a portfolio of articles, videos and photographs.

"Of course, we really appreciate your help," said Kai. "So we'd like you to manage us and take you along to Cote D'Ivoire if we're successful." That was more like it. Sadly, they didn't submit their application in time, so it never came to anything.

Before leaving, the marabout told me the medicine was very powerful and there would be side effects. We returned home and for the next three days I lay in bed, feverish, with blinding headaches and vomiting.

I hoped it was worth it.

Not long after, I revisited the tiny village where once upon a time on my first trip to the Casamance I slept on the side of the road and was woken by a goat licking my face. Khady had been visiting her sister there and I'd gone to pick her up.

We arrived and I had an inkling how the Beatles must have felt as the entire village crowded around to look, prod and poke me. Many had barely seen a whitey before. A far cry from my previous visit, when only the goat had shown interest. After lunch, I wanted to head back, to arrive home before dark, but Khady said there was an important sacred forest nearby and we should take the opportunity to be blessed and protected. I've been "protected" so much I should be invincible. We walked off through the warm rain, down a sandy track into rice fields and the forest beyond, followed like the Pied Piper by a large gossip of women.

The forest was sacred for females and the site of their initiations. They made an exception for *Johnny Toubab*, but upon arrival I was ordered to strip. I looked around at the 30 or 40 women, ranging from Grandmas to young girls and thought, no thanks, I don't want to do that. They accepted that I left my boxers on and then led Khady, who was wrapped in a sarong, and me deep into a jungle grove where a large gnarled tree grew.

There was a lump growing from the tree that had been smoothed after years of offerings of milk and what appeared to be blood. We crouched in the gloom and all shut our eyes, raised our palms to the air and chanted. My name was repeated regularly. Then we crumbled biscuits and poured milk onto the fetish. When they stopped, I said, "*amine*" and fluttered my hands to the sky.

Khady told me the tree was home to a very powerful genie and it was excellent that I had made the offering. I would now have good luck with my work. A few days later, I heard that the publisher was interested in this book.

Back in Abene, I decided, as I am wont to do occasionally, to stroll in the forest near my house to look for snakes. I met a man with a spade who was digging up roots for African traditional medicine. He slammed the spade into a vine hanging between us. White sap spurted out which he told me cures bladder problems. Maybe it does; I have studied pharmacology and many modern drugs are derived from natural sources.

Some natural medicines are used in regular ways such as herbs drunk as a tea or as an oil rubbed into the skin. Others are less obvious and used to wash the body and drive out spirits: soap resembling cow dung and buckets of herbs and twigs in water that smells of rotten eggs. Or as talismanic charms: almost every time I check a pocket in my camera bag or backpack, I find a seed or leather amulet that Khady has placed there for my further protection.

African traditional medicine seems to work side by side with the gris-gris, offering both protection and cure from ailments. Africans believe that Western medicine is good and will cure an illness or wound, but it won't cure the underlying reason for receiving that problem; perhaps a curse from a witch, devil or a jealous person. For that, the local medicine and a marabout is required.

Khady told me that there are many girls in Abene who want a toubab and they are not happy that I've not chosen them. Therefore, they're trying to cause me problems by putting curses on me, hence the multiple accidents I've had, two quite serious during my first few months here. One bus, one motorbike, one boat and three cars. None of my African friends have had so many accidents in their entire lives and it's not typical for this part of the world.

Following a trip to photograph a ceremony in a remote village, I became a little sick with fever. I attributed this to some water I drank out of a bin. It was nothing serious and didn't cause me any concern, but then I'm the sort of person who has to lose a limb before I grumble.

The reason I write this is to highlight the different attitude of Africans to illness. On that occasion four different people have told me they didn't sleep as they were so worried about me. I was given three different traditional medications. Khady wanted me to go to the hospital. Her marabout came round to give me a back massage. I vomited halfway through and felt fine after. Then I had to pour a green leafy liquid over me which smelt lovely, but left me picking bits of green from my body for days.

It seems most Africans are hypochondriacs and worry far more than I do. I put the main reason for the concern down to the fact that people here do tend to just die for apparently no reason or following minor illnesses that would be trivial in the West. People can't afford modern medicine which is relatively expensive, so leave illnesses too long. Also, they don't have the routine checkups that would highlight concerns like we do in the UK.

When I become sick, I'll typically think back over my food and drink sources from the previous 24 hours to explain the cause. Khady and her family were more concerned with who had provided them to me and why. The traditional medicines are more for my protection than to cure the illness. Whether the medicine works or not is beside the point. The placebo effect is strong, and mixed with local belief, people do wither and die if they don't take them.

Although sceptical of black magic, odd things do happen to me. One day Binta, the shop keeper, came to visit. After some small talk, she revealed her real reason for the visit, which was a follow-up to our previous conversation about "jiggy jiggy boom boom" in Ziguinchor. Clearly I hadn't been forceful enough in my rejection of her, so, upon hearing that Khady was in another village visiting family, she tried again.

"So, Simon, it is surely true that you love me very much. I know that. You know that. Any time you visit me in my home, we can make the thing. You know, the jiggy thing. It'll be our secret, we won't tell no one."

Again I politely declined. Hours later I had a shooting pain in my lower back. The next day I had to give up on a walk to the village and return home, limping slowly and pausing in agony. I've never had a back problem in my life. A friend who knew about the woman's visit told me it was clearly a curse. I was popped on the back of a motorbike and trundled off to a nearby village to see a healer.

She gave me a good massage and a selection of wood, roots and birds' nests to boil up and shower with as protection against the curse. Finally, for full protection and recovery I was told I must prepare some rice and fish for the local kids. This is the fun part of the process. Often we have a gaggle of laughing, snotty and dusty kids, excitedly playing with Gulliver and hungrily gathering around a bowl of something we've prepared. On an economic and community level, this also makes sense: protection from spells feeds local children who might not have enough to eat at home.

A few months later, fully healed, I met Binta again. Khady always warns me not to shake people's hands unless they are friends. This time, before I had time to think, Binta had taken my hand in hers. As I walked away, the pain returned, just for an hour or so. Is there something subliminal going on?

I'm not sure. I know I don't really believe it's mystical, but it does make a great story.

Not too many weeks go by without hearing a similar tale, some of them utterly fantastical, but believed without question by most people. For example, we met one of Khady's friends who told us the story of when she met the devil at the crossroads in the Gambia. Khady tells me we can never go there between 1am and 5am, not that I'm likely to.

This crossroads is known as the traffic light as it's the only traffic light in the nation. The girl told us about how she was working in a tourist bar and travelled home very late in a friend's taxi. As they pulled up at the light, a man was standing by the side of the road. She looked close and saw that he had really odd, big eyes, like a cat, and they glowed red. As he swung his arms, the shirt rode up revealing fur-covered arms. She went to speak and he raised a finger to his lips, shushing her.

Two months later, she woke up in a village where they were treating her with traditional medicine, and said she'd just been released from a hospital having been in a coma. She said she went back to the hospital and looked at the notes to see if this was true. Sure enough, she'd been in the hospital in a coma for the past two months and as they were unable to treat her they had released her to her marabout, whose powers had cured what Western-style medicine was unable to.

Spiritual beliefs underlie many of the traditional dances and ceremonies. I first experienced the *Koumpo* dance when

I was visiting a remote area for Khady's father's follow-up ceremony 40 days after his death. For a couple of days, I had sat staring into the middle distance, drinking tea and messing around with the kids. Then I heard chanting. I followed a procession into a forest clearing where several hundred people formed a large circle. Men waved sticks and chanted. Women banged together two bits of metal and sang. A drum group pounded a beat. Many men were dressed as women, apparently to bring luck to infertile women.

People stepped into the circle, strutted across to a member of the opposite sex, shook a leg, then quickly turned and ran back. If a woman doesn't respond after three approaches, she is uninterested. As the sole toubab, I received some attention. A rather large woman in an AC/DC T-shirt thrust her pelvis, bounced her hefty *jaifonday* off me – nearly knocking me over – and ran away laughing.

Then the *Koumpo* arrived, or rather three *Koumpos*. A *Koumpo* is a dancer, covered in green reeds, who can twirl like a crazy tumbleweed and seemingly elongate itself to 10 feet tall. It arrives when a message needs to be given to the community and it disciplines young people and provides rules.

Next, *Essamaye* arrived, an Ewok-like monkey devil, and *N'yass* the black ape – masked dancers who discipline children and scare evil spirits. If the kids were scared of the *Koumpo*, they were positively terrified of these creatures, which chased them with sticks.

As I watched *N'yass*, a lad whispered in my ear that we have these in England. I told him that, no, we don't have gorillas in England.

"Are you sure? I saw them in a film. One carried a girl to the top of the building."

"King Kong?"

"Yes, kinky kong."

I then saw something I'd heard about but never thought I'd see. A large sweating man was working himself up into a trance, eyes rolling back into his head, spinning and gyrating wildly. He pulled a large knife from a sheath, demonstrated its razor sharpness before slicing his arms and stabbing himself in the torso. As he did this, another guy was sprinkling herbally medicated water on him. The gris-gris did protect him and he had not a scratch. Diola elders have confided in me that as a tribe they have been opening bodies and performing successful medical operations for years before learning the methods of the white man.

Later, Khady asked if I'd been scared of the *Koumpo*, as I'd gone close to take a picture.

"Well, they're just dancers, right?"

"You think so? I don't. They're from the forest. How can they be human? Africa is very dark. We cannot understand everything."

One of the family heads was the personal doctor to the Gambian president. He corroborated that the *Koumpo* was a forest spirit. I wasn't quite sure if he was serious or having a laugh at my expense.

Later on back in Abene, I heard that a friend, Papis, had organised a *Koumpo* dance for a tour group. I went along, thinking it would be a toned-down tourist version, but although it was on a smaller scale, the dance was the same.

I showed Khady some photographs later. In one, a face was clearly visible amongst the *Koumpo's* reeds.

"Maybe this man didn't believe and the *Koumpo* ate him," she said.

I saw my mechanic one day, driving through the village in a customer's car. He stopped, jumping out to greet me. The car carried on, lumbering forward into a shop, knocking over a stand.

He laughed, shouting no problem. "It's God's will."

"God's will that you forgot to put the handbrake on?"

"No, no, it's not my fault, it's God's will."

What a great life view, not having to take responsibility for anything. He is now my ex-mechanic.

Belief is perhaps my biggest conflict; myself a biology graduate non-believer and Khady a superstitious Muslim. I have such a strong sense of wonder of the world and of the science behind it, of which knowledge is increasing all the time, that to reduce life to "God created it" seems to me massively simplistic.

Beliefs of all kinds are very different in Africa, for example equal opportunities for women and views on homosexuality. I feel that in the UK at least, we've evolved enough so that these days you have to work hard to be, for example, sexist or homophobic. But I'm aware that this is my toubab mentality.

I have met many well-educated, western-valued Africans who are horrified if I suggest gays should not be punished, even executed, or that God may be a human invention. There simply isn't a discussion around these matters. African society has not had the history the West has over the past few hundred years that has caused many to question their religion or the history of the past few decades surrounding equal opportunities in all its forms. Africa's different and therefore I can make a distinction and roll with it.

A point many commentators seem to miss is the importance we place upon the individual in the West and the rights and choices attached to that person. In Africa, this is not so important and a person is viewed in terms of their relationships with others, for example as a brother or sister, a father or mother, son or daughter, a Chief, a Diola, a Muslim and so on. All of these relationships carry obligations that are considered more important than anything an individual might prefer had he or she been given a free choice. The right to an education instead of working for the family or the right of a man to practise homosexuality rather than marry and produce children. The happiness of the individual is considered less important than the well-being of the community, and failure to maintain the traditions of the ancestors is thought to bring bad luck.

I'd never survive here without an open attitude but one thing that does make me chuckle is when other toubabs can reconcile their religious beliefs and yet laugh at some of the more superstitious beliefs of local people. We all believe what we want to believe.

Incidentally, I've only ever met one African, a guide in the Dogon country of Mali, who claimed not to be religious. When I questioned him further he explained he did of course believe in God, but didn't subscribe to any organised religion.

That seems like a good start.

BOILY BOILY

I am lying down, sweat trickling into my eyes and ears. Sometimes it feels too hot to breathe. There is not an air conditioning unit in sight. Any cold drink warms up before I can finish it. If I'm not smothering on the sun cream, I'm slapping on the jungle formula. Despite precautions, I have 10 egg-sized lumps across my back that itch like fury. Last week I thought I had malaria: I was in a restaurant and came over feverish and nauseous, head spinning, stars in front of my eyes. In retrospect I reckon the copious quantities of gin and tonic the day before and exhaustion in the muggy 45° heat might have played a part.

The development of our land and our life continued throughout the hot, steamy rainy season. I had dug an African-style long-drop toilet but one day it was no longer there. The ground had subsided in the heavy rains and there was just a big collapsed hole of mud. I suppose it's a measure of how relaxed I'd become that I simply thought, "Oh bugger", then carried on with whatever I was doing.

The rains were bad. There were days when, after a short rainfall, an open bin of at least one metre tall would be full. I'd pour it away and an hour later it would be full again.

The track on our land which we drove on everyday had become compacted through use, but to either side it was quicksand. One night I was in bed listening to the wind howling. I looked out of the window to rather worryingly see the palm trees almost bent down to the ground. I got back into bed and lay there wondering if the roof was about to blow off.

Before the rains, when the ground is driest, I was planting trees and flowers into parched sands, sure they'd never survive. By the time we reached August, deep into the rainy season, the water table had risen level with the ground, as had the water in the well – I was tempted to jump in and tread water every now and again as it was so hot. I just needed to stamp on the ground and water seeped out. This wasn't good news for the new concrete floor of our house. It was constantly damp and I made a few holes where I trod a little heavily. We had to put a delay on digging the waste pit for the new toilet in order to wait for the water level to go down and so had to use the neighbour's loo instead.

I worked almost every day, but in short bursts. The heat and humidity sapped my energy. It was, as they say in Diola, "boily boily".

Generally, I can take the heat. It's the humidity that's the killer, especially when working. I would soak my travel towel in cold water and tie it around my head. When the sun was beating down at full blast, it was as if somebody had taken a heavy blanket, soaked it in boiling water, twisted it around and given me a thorough whacking around the head.

I checked the BBC weather website to discover it was 36°C with 90 percent humidity. The humidity made it feel much hotter. I'm not a good judge of temperature, though. When I was in Siberia, it was -30° although to me it felt like a mere -20°.

There were occasional days where I simply lay lethargically in the hammock, sighing every time a small gust of slightly cooler warm air hit me. It's far too hot to wear protective clothing, so I usually worked in a pair of shorts and flip flops. It's backbreaking work hacking at spiky, thorny and sometimes poisonous plants that are crawling with insects.

I usually manage 40 minutes to an hour, by which time I am covered in sweat, dirt, biting ants and have thorns in the soles of my feet and blood running down my legs. I would then sit in the shade puffing and panting, downing gallons of water. If it's been a really tough day, Khady will disappear to the shop and return with ice and cans of coke. At times like this it truly is the real thing.

The other problem with the humidity is when clothes and bedding get damp. I hung up a shirt that I'd been wearing. It must have been very slightly damp with sweat. I then put my overcoat over the shirt and left it for a week. For reasons known only to myself, I have a Ben Sherman black overcoat. Perfect for looking stylish in the British winter, slowly rotting here. There was a strong damp smell, so I opened the coat and saw the shirt beneath covered in a white fungal powder. It had only been hanging for a week.

I suffered somewhat with raw blisters all over my chest and back. They were diagnosed as a bacterial infection and I was given antibiotics, but doctors here give antibiotics for everything. Gulliver had had chicken pox a couple of weeks earlier and my illness bore all the symptoms of shingles. It certainly hurt like hell and I barely slept. I'll tell you one thing: accidentally spraying 50 percent DEET on open wounds didn't help. I danced like a monkey on fire.

Then I was laid up for a week with a raging fever, spending nights lying on up to four towels, all of which were drenched by morning. I went to two hospitals; the first wouldn't test me for malaria and said I had flu. I spoke to a toubab who warned me that maybe they thought they'd make more money selling flu medications than for a malaria test, or maybe they had only one or two test kits left. Medical advice is always to test for malaria in West Africa when fever is present, especially in the rainy season, so I wanted to set my mind at ease.

The second hospital confirmed that I didn't have malaria, just a serious case of man-flu. I now realise I've probably never had flu before as this was much worse than any cold I've had in my life. I've managed to spend more than six years in tropical Asia and five years in Africa and I have never had malaria. Khady's been here her whole life and has never had it.

The doctor was friendly and told me about his Californian wife. Then as I stepped out to lie down and rest on a concrete slab for a while, he propositioned Khady and told her he loved her, despite never having met her before. She returned to me, angry, muttering "Africa, oh Africa ..."

We normally work in the early morning and late afternoon and if we don't take a siesta we'll often visit the beach. Gulliver likes the water so one day we all went down to lie in the surf. Khady stood on something that slithered from under her foot which I said was probably a fish. A friend, Ibby, was nearby with a machete. He ran down and stabbed at the water. Minutes later he hauled a one-metre-width manta ray from the water which was promptly thrown into in the back of Kermit. That evening I hacked it up, which was difficult as the skin was sandpaper rough, like a shark. After throwing the guts and so on into the forest for our resident monitor lizards Morris and Stumpy, I lit a fire and grilled it slowly over hot coals. Surprisingly, it tasted like very tender grilled lamb and went well with a marinade of onion, mustard, lemon juice and chilli.

To help out on the land, we employed a Gambian lad called Fakeba, who helped me with watering, security and general maintenance. He's incredibly handy – it doesn't matter what I ask, he knows how to do it to a reasonable standard. He's a trained mechanic, knows how to look after ducks, can mend a fence, put a straw roof on a house and grow tomatoes. He's one of those people who gives you a look when you're trying to do something as if to say: "Why are you bothering, let me do it properly." Which is just what I need.

I decided to build a wardrobe. Now, this may surprise you,

but Abene has a branch of Ikea. It's called the jungle and I went shopping with my machete. A couple of days later and I'd built us a wooden wardrobe. Come to think of it, that's quicker than some of the flat packs I've put together. It may not be to everyone's taste, but I was pleased and liked the rustic look. There were so many jobs I wanted to do, but I had to slow down. Between about 10am and 4pm it was just too hot, and every time I attempted to do anything, my eyeballs felt like they were boiling, sweat poured from me, my face was rubbed raw from my towel and every single mosquito bite started itching again. Maybe tomorrow?

Life began to feel a bit like an endurance test, although I knew it would get better when the house was finished and dried out and I could store everything properly. Frogs jumping out of my bag every time I reach for a T-shirt couldn't last forever, surely? I suffered from prickly heat, which is like being stabbed in the face by knitting needles as somebody tickles you.

The number and variety of insects is astounding. As dusk fell, swarms of mosquitoes gnawed at our knuckles. Every time a light was switched on was an excuse for a bug party. I spent most of the day dripping with sweat and the insides of my arms grew sore from rubbing damp against the table as I wrote. Due to the insects, we had to eat our evening meal before dark, then retire to the bedroom under mosquito nets. The numerous geckos must have thought it was Christmas.

I'd be lying if there weren't times I wondered if I was doing the right thing. Shouldn't I be back in England moaning about commuting, reality television and the cold? Then one day the rains stopped. The sun shone brightly, illuminating more shades of green than I ever knew existed, a rainbow appeared and I looked at Khady and Gulliver who never seemed to stop laughing. I realised I was as happy as I'd ever been.

We keep a succession of pets at the Little Baobab, but Africa is tough for animals and we had some bad luck.

The first was Toubab, a small and very cute white puppy. Somebody from Khady's home village gave him to us. He threw up all the way home in Kermit and then we discovered he was full of ticks and fleas, but we gave him a saucer of milk and bits of fish and he quickly grew into a fine little dog. Over the next couple of months, Toubab became part of our family, growing from not much bigger than my hand into a small yapping dog who craved attention and loved to chase me around the garden. Perhaps it wasn't the best timing in the world to get a new puppy 10 days before having a baby, but I never regretted it, even when he destroyed my shirt as I crouched to light a fire.

One day, we went to stay with Khady's uncle in Bignona. When we woke up the following morning, Toubab was gone. He'd escaped from a small enclosure in the garden. He never strayed far, but the kids searched the local neighbourhood and our conclusion was he'd been dognapped. Everybody loved Toubab – he was well fed, well loved and looked much healthier than your typical mangy African mutt. The marabout told us if we fed some chickens, he would return. I fed some chickens, but on this occasion the marabout was wrong.

As I joined in the search, walking through compounds and down sand tracks, the mild humour I'd employed in naming him faded as I was greeted everywhere by cries of "toubab". I couldn't stand it, so returned to the uncle's house. We never did find him.

Our chickens faired little better. Initially. We started off with two, Tarzan and Jane. They turned out to be Tarzan and John, so there weren't as many chicks as we hoped. They were low maintenance and foraged about the land.

Then one day, we were awoken by an almighty kerfuffle at six in the morning. Khady ran out and chased a dog for a mile down the track. He had John in his jaws. She returned holding the poor, twitching fellow. We tried to give him some food and water, but half an hour later he went to the great farm in the sky.

Tarzan, the remaining chicken, gained a parasite that infested the whole house. We were all crawling with tiny bugs. They didn't bite, but you could feel them crawling all over. We had three options: buy some petrol and scrub him; take him to the beach for a swim in seawater; cook roast chicken.

He was delicious.

Since those early dark days of chicken husbandry, things have thankfully improved. We built a large chicken house from banku bricks and now have 20 or so more, along with several ducks and pigeons.

Not long after Toubab disappeared, I was feeling a little sorry for myself as we grilled fish on the fire. Khady beckoned me over and told me to bring a torch. Peering from the darkness was a kitten, just a tiny wriggle of bones. She was shivering, flea ridden, scared and starving. We flicked some fish in its direction and gave it a saucer of milk. The kitten was still there the next day, and the next. We thought she was orphaned and I like to think the local animals told it if you go to the house with the green car, they're not too bad and will feed you. So, we had yet another addition to the family, whom we named "Jaifonday", although she didn't have much of one (in case you forgot, jaifonday means large African bum). Later, she disappeared as abruptly as she arrived.

Not long after, I felt dizzy, started burning up and my head was buzzing. I resembled a tomato with a face. Checking my well-thumbed copy of *Where There is No Doctor* (a manual for aid workers) I decided it was heat rash, so not much to worry about. Occasionally I liked to visit a nearby hollow baobab tree that is home to a number of bats and lizards. Khady didn't like me visiting this or other big trees as she believes they're homes to genies. After this illness she could take no more and called over elder relatives who gave me stern warnings and reiterated that there are mystical things in Africa that I should take seriously.

"It's very dark and there are some things you will never understand ..."

Apparently, the genie didn't like me visiting the tree and was sending me a warning by making me look like something with a big red head. My big tree exploration days were over.

Just as I'd vowed not to visit the tree, our adopted daughter Jumbo came running to us at breakfast.

"Quick, Jaifonday's in the tree."

We ran around to look but everyone was too scared to get close. Khady warned me to keep back. It might not be Jaifonday, it could be a genie who's taken the form of Jaifonday, she explained. From a distance, I could see a little white head peering at me, but it was too gloomy to really tell. I wasn't allowed to crawl in to find out – Khady said it was full of black mambas, which was a decent enough deterrent, even for me. I suggested leaving some fish at the entrance and waiting to see if she reappeared.

About three weeks later a friend recognised Jaif at a nearby house and brought her back, followed by a procession of kids all chanting "Jai-jai-fonday ... jai-jai-jai-fonday." We had our cat back. I enquired about her having been in the tree.

"Maybe it was a good genie giving us a message that Jaif is safe," said Khady. There's an answer for everything. Then the kitten ran away again. Periodically we'd catch glimpses of her through the trees, now a wild cat. Perhaps she always was.

Various other animals came our way, as it appeared we had the reputation as the local animal sanctuary. Scrappy was a particularly mangy little mutt, from Madina Dafe, Khady's home village. He was a friendly chap, and once the insects dropped off, he started growing. Before Africa, I'd never kept a dog and didn't know about castration. When Scrappy was about 10 months old, Fakeba declared we should do this. It was true that he was skulking off each evening, breaking through newly maintained fences at frustratingly frequent intervals, returning with ever deeper wounds gouged into his flanks from fights with other dogs. I wanted to do it, but felt it was too late. He was quite big and if we'd do this, it needed to be done properly, not with a rusty razor blade in the forest, as was the custom.

One day Khady walked into our house, ashen-faced. Fakeba and Bakary had cut Scrappy. He was crouched in the forest, looking miserable, although quite frankly, so would I if someone had cut my bollocks off. I had sharp words with Fakeba. Secretly, I thought that perhaps, assuming that Scrappy recovered, this was for the best, although I wasn't happy that he'd ignored what Khady and I had said. Scrappy did perk up the next day and in less than a week seemed back to normal, minus the nocturnal escapes.

We were having a run of bad luck at this point and Khady was keen to provide more spiritual protection for the Little Baobab. After a visit to the marabout, she tied a snake's head above our front door, although it didn't last long as something ate it. It wasn't me, honest. We fed porridge to the local kids in an act of charity that should have brought good fortune, but that was not enough. She returned to the marabout and came back with a bag of herbs, leaves and bits of wood, then declared she had to perform a ritual with this at the gate at midnight, naked. I pressed for further details and asked to be the photographer, but both requests were denied. She performed the ceremony and told me we'd have good luck now. Then Scrappy died.

It was a month or two after the castration and I thought he was fully recovered. In the past week, something hadn't been quite right, though, and he'd had a strange look in his eye. I had popped to Ziguinchor for the weekend and when I returned, Khady said the previous day he'd coughed up blood, laid down and died. She thought he'd been infected by some kind of insect, but we'll never know for sure.

Ramadan had ended and I'd performed reasonably well. For three weeks I drank only water through the day and held out till the sunset for my evening meal. I wasn't even too ravenous, as my stomach was shrinking. I'm not exactly big, but weight dripped off and my six-pack made a mid-life reappearance. I thought Khady would be impressed, but attitudes are different in Africa.

"People will think I don't feed you. I don't like."

Then, one morning when I felt hungry and I was wondering what variation of fish and rice we'd have that night, I drove past the French-run restaurant. Gerard, the proprietor, had hand-painted a new menu outside and I noticed hamburgers, a new addition. Why did he do this during Ramadan? It was as if it was just to tempt me.

The previous evening, we'd eaten rice with palm oil. This is a red oil that tends to cause diarrhoea, but is popular; we ate it with mushy boiled fish. The night before we'd had *maffe*. This brown slimy sauce looks like diarrhoea but doesn't cause it. I asked if we could have vegetables, but Khady said the builders didn't like them. For 10 days, all I had eaten was fish and rice, with a slightly different sauce. Moreover, I knew I had it coming for the next 10 days at least. I used to like fish.

So, once I'd gotten hamburgers into my head they wouldn't leave. I guiltily told Gerard I was taking a break from Ramadan and ordered an ice-cold Gazelle beer and a burger. He told me there were no hamburgers. It was too late to turn back – the beer was open – so I settled for steak and chips. I opened my book and had a very pleasant couple of hours on the verandah reading, eating and drinking. Gerard wasn't taking part in Ramadan either: he called out, raised a glass of pastis to me and we both smiled guiltily as his thirsty wife looked on.

Towards the end of Ramadan, some *Baye Fall* guys who run a café in the village started blasting devotional music at ear-slitting volume day and night. With this and the heat, neither Khady or I slept much and even she, a Muslim, was fed up.

"God doesn't demand this," she muttered. "They're selfish and we can't say anything as it's Islam."

She is starting to think like a toubab.

I had some sympathy though as they were lovely guys and just following their tradition. Besides, it was Ibrahima, the Baye Fall guy in Dakar, who had given me my first gris-gris and set me off on this new life.

I was keen to understand a bit more about them and chatted to my neighbour Chérif Mané (no relation), who is *Baye Fall*.

The *Baye Fall* holy men of Senegal are as distinctive as the *Saddhu* holy men in India and are fairly similar in appearance, minus the nudity. I first came across a couple of them with begging bowls, patchwork robes, beads and dread locks on the streets of downtown Dakar. They asked for change, which I didn't have.

"That's okay, perhaps you can buy me some food in this shop?" one said, hopefully.

I'm okay with that. I was thinking he wanted a few pennies for a bread roll, but when he demanded nearly £50 for a sack of rice and a sack of sugar I chuckled and went along my way.

The *Baye Fall* Brotherhood is a Sufi Islamic sect founded

by Mame Cheikh Ibrahima Fall – "the Light". He met Sufi Cheikh Ahmadou Bamba who was protesting the colonialism of the French, in 1892, and became his disciple. Whilst in orthodox Islam, every follower is directly in touch with Allah, in Senegal, relationships with God are mostly channeled through various religious leaders. Cheikh Amadou Bamba, the founder of the *Mouride* Brotherhood, is an iconic figure in Senegal. His name and portrait are painted on buildings, stickers, taxi windows, necklaces, and T-shirts. Every February, more than two million followers go to Touba, a holy city in Senegal, where Bamba lived, worked and died. This event, the Grand *Magal*, celebrates the leader's return from exile in 1907 after having been banished for 20 years by the French.

According to my neighbour, the Brotherhood's mission is similar to the sun and the moon. It has never stopped from beginning of creation until today. Whatever gives nausea to the vulture makes the hyena vomit; if it comes to the *Baye Fall*, they will purify it. This is typical of the types of conversation I have on a daily basis. Still, it beats talking about the weather.

Baye Fall is being at one with one's energy, through devotion and action, undertaking all work as prayer. Sometimes, as I had experienced, they own nothing and beg. Instead of Islamic rituals such as fasting and prayer, they perform hard labour. They sing all night in a circle and rotate counter-clockwise, the key into "the other time". The circle is the journey back to oneself. There is no beginning, no end. There is only one.

A short while after Ramadan was the Islamic festival of *Tabaski*, which fell towards the end of the rains. This is a time when every family, if they have the means, buys and slaughters a sheep as an offering to God. You eat a third, give a third to extended family members and the final third to the poor. In nearby Bignona, I drove down the road where farmers had brought their sheep to sell. There were literally thousands of animals enacting a biblical scene with wizened old shepherds dressed in turbans and robes, carrying wooden staffs. According to the Koran, if you don't have the financial means you can do a chicken or fish instead but it seems people here haven't read that bit. I was asked by several people to buy them a sheep, which costs about £100. If God doesn't provide, maybe the toubab will.

Given my expenditure that year and the fact that I'm not a Muslim, I didn't buy a sheep. That was me applying Western logic, of course. I did have the means, even if it meant leaving myself with nothing for the next month. This is the perpetual financial issue for a toubab in Senegal as saving, investment and the concept of insurance (in terms of having an emergency fund) are unknown ideas for most Africans, who struggle to make ends meet on a day-to-day basis. I struggled to explain this to my friend Bass. He couldn't understand why tourists wouldn't pay a couple of quid for one of his shirts, then he'd see them drinking an ice-cold drink, a luxury most Africans can't afford.

Instead of a sheep, we bought some very tasty beef. I cooked it for several hours over hot coals. Later, we walked around the village greeting everyone, all dressed up in their finest *boubous*. By the time we'd eaten deliciously tender lamb in a peppery sauce night after night, I became so sick of it I was glad I didn't have a whole sheep to get through.

As a *Tabaski* gift, a marabout gave me a tail. This was a gris-gris-like charm that he attached to my car keys. I'm not sure what animal it was from, but it was still attached to something rather pungent. I reckon any vet worth his salt could have brought it back to life.

The great fence of Abene was just about finished; all we needed now was a gate. I designed a wooden one and thought a natural finish would look good, but Khady suggested painting it.

"What colour," I asked?

"Yellow, green and red," she suggested. The Senegalese flag and reggae colours.

Perfect. I was very proud of my reggae gate, but the posts made by our builders were crumbling and so the gate was a bit wonky. I tried repairing it several times, but there are some things you can't polish, so I built some fancy brick posts to match the house. I always say a fancy gate needs fancy posts. I cemented in the hinges, hung the gates, wedged everything with bricks and put up a palm-leaf barrier to make it obvious the gate was not in use yet. Then I nipped out for an hour. I came back to find the palms strewn on the ground and the gate half open with both hinges torn from the semi-dry cement. I punched the post, which made my knuckles bleed.

Given that we had a fence built of natural materials, I knew it would require maintenance but had hoped it would give a year or two's good service first. But it appears that palms are a popular food with the local ants and in many places they had stripped it bare, leaving big holes. Goats completed the job and came in to feed on our carefully planted, watered and cared-for flowers and orange trees.

"This is Africa," I muttered through gritted teeth whilst trying to patch it up. Khady had been on at me to put some barbed wire around the perimeter. No, let's keep it natural, said the naïve toubab, thinking of both aesthetics and his wallet. In the event, I came up with a better solution: lining the fence with fishing net that adds strength and integrity, and then growing a spindly cactus-like plant all the way around, that I hope will grow into a natural hedge.

I thought the rains had finished. It hadn't rained in nearly two weeks, so I spent a long Sunday morning pulling water from the well and drenching all the orange, banana and avocado trees. Exhausting work. Just as I'd finished, I looked up to see pitch-black clouds which promptly opened. It continued to rain all afternoon and evening.

I may be painting a rather damp, soggy and miserable picture of the rainy season, but in reality I love it. The landscapes are beautiful as the orange dust is washed back into the earth and everything becomes green with more shades than I could ever imagine. At night, we are treated to the greatest show on earth. As I recline in my traditional African chair, I stare up at the starry night sky to see flashes of lightening every two or three seconds showcasing the sky in all directions. It is magical.

Around this time, something flattering happened. Whilst strolling around, Khady and I ran into her cousin, a very shiny, happy Chérif Big Man. He's always smiley and I always greet him as "*petit homme*", whilst he cries "Big Man" at me. His girlfriend had just given birth to their first son. The name? Simon Goudiaby.

The next day, a very shiny, happy Bakary arrived at our compound. Without knowing about Little Simon, he told us his wife had just delivered a little girl ... Khady Badje.

So the following week we attended baptism ceremonies for both Simon and Khady. Surreal. According to rumours, there may be further Simons on their way in the village. One of my goals in life has always been to start a cult, so this could be a good start.

COOLY COOLY

I am back and I feel strange. It is cold and wet. Wounds that have been weeping for weeks, unable to heal in the tropical climate, dry out within hours. Most tourists return to England with a mask or a drum. I arrive at Heathrow in a hot and feverish sweat with a scar, a wonky elbow and something living in my hand. Still, most tourist souvenirs are tacky.

The rains were coming to an end when an emergency came up in the UK and I had to return to sign some legal papers.

Normally when I travel, I have weeks if not months, to prepare. This time, I had a short, sharp reverse shock, not only culturally but physically. Senegal was boily boily; at the end of the rainy season, the heat builds every day to a resounding crescendo and life was, quite frankly, feeling uncomfortably hot. Europe meanwhile, was chilly chilly.

A slightly worried man at Banjul airport, called Moussa, wanted to chat.

"I have heard that in England it sometimes goes below 20°." he said. "I would surely die if that is the case."

I was starting to think I might, too.

So, on Friday morning I was sweating in the back of a bush taxi and on Saturday morning I was sitting frozen in Frankfurt airport, the first time I'd seen the naughty side of 30° in a year.

I left Abene in a jeep, driving the 10 or so miles down sandy tracks through forest, emerging at the river separating Senegal from Gambia. There was a dug-out canoe waiting and it was a short ride to border control and Customs where I bribed the official to let me through. I threw my rucksack on a small cart towed by a donkey, jumped on after it and off we trotted, up to the bus station, from where I took a *geli-geli* (minibus) to Banjul airport.

Along the way, we were pulled over by the police and a man in a green safari suit sporting a magnificent Afro. He turned to the police officer stating "this is a perfect example of an environmental hazard," before telling the driver of the *geli-geli* he would not inconvenience the passengers, but that he must report straight to the police station after this trip. As we pulled away, the driver told us it was Gambia's justice minister.

I was early, so stayed on the bus for a few miles past the airport, where I was dropped off on the roadside. I walked a couple of miles down a sandy track through mangroves to Lamin lodge. This is a wooden structure overlooking a *bolong* (stream) from the Gambia River that offers superb views and decent food in a structure that could well be Tarzan's treehouse. I love it here and picked up some tips for my own dwelling. I relaxed, eating oyster stew, taking in the view and enjoying some quiet moments in Africa before my trip to England.

The journey from Abene in Senegal to Banjul airport in Gambia can take half a day and costs me pennies. From Heathrow I paid about 20 times more to a bus company for a 45-minute ride. Welcome to Britain. Okay, so I had a double seat, the windscreen wasn't smashed and we left on time, but it was boring; I'd gotten rather fond of things shitting on me as I travel. I realise some people do want Wifi, electrical connections and computerised screens, but it seems we're all having to pay first-class prices whether we want a first-class service or not. I think if I had continued to live in the UK I would have turned into a grumpy old man.

Everywhere I went I noted people insulating themselves from their surroundings with technology: iPads, smart phones, headphones. I'd spent all year reading about recession and austerity in Europe. I know that in comparison to recent years, people are struggling and that I can't compare the standard of living to that in Africa. But I couldn't help wondering how Khady would be viewing this, had she been able to come with me. Given the queues in every shop I visited, the number of new and always busy-coffee shops and so on, I think she'd be bewildered by the notion that toubabs are struggling.

I discussed my new life with friends and family. Amongst other thoughts, they were bemused and slightly baffled as to why I'd want to deny myself items like electricity, running water and cheese. As I'm wont to do, I started musing on why this might be.

In Africa it is often the simplest things that are so hard. Things that in Europe would barely be worthy of comment, here involve a major campaign. It was similar back in the mid-1990s in Vietnam where I remember devoting an entire Sunday to buying a tin opener. In Africa, if I want a shower, I have to walk to the well, draw the water and then gasp as it's so damn hot and the water's so cold. If I want to buy something beyond basic staple items, I have to travel a hundred miles to Ziguinchor, go to another country, the Gambia, or go without.

I've made my peace with this and feel happier for it. I'm not a Luddite, I have a computer, a Kindle and a camera. But I've also grown weary of a culture where everything is so easy and accessible at the click of a button. As a teenager I'd scour mail-order catalogues for rare records. Almost any book you can wish for online negates the need to spend weekends rummaging through second-hand bookshops. When I was a lad, I'd be excited for months in the lead up to Christmas. Literally not sleeping, sometimes dreaming of something quite simple, such as a history encyclopedia.

The joy of receiving an item never exceeded the excitement of its anticipation, and it still doesn't.

I now simply prefer to do without much of the time and look forward to certain luxuries. A cold beer at the end of an arduous 36-hour bus trip. Steak and chips after six weeks of fish and rice. A decent internet connection every few weeks when popping to the city. Monsoonal rains after months of rising heat and humidity. The challenges of finding items, improvising or simply doing without makes life more interesting for me. I also have to be really sure I want and need something before I go ahead. This is not the life for an impulse shopper.

I landed at Banjul airport and it was good to be back home. It was also reassuring to feel like I was really "returning home". I had felt this way when I first laid eyes on Khady with our "bump", but in the intervening months I had truly put down roots – not only metaphorically, but literally. I'd travelled to Britain on a one-way ticket, unsure of how long I'd be, but I completed my business and managed to get back in just under a week. In that time, the weather in Abene had changed and there was now a refreshing chill in the air in the mornings and evenings. Even in the middle of the day, although hot, it was possible to work without breaking into a sweat.

I thought I'd arrive back without incident. This being Africa, there was bound to be an incident though, wasn't there? To reach the Senegal border, I waited for hours in a packed bus that had been overloaded on the roof. I used to be relaxed about such things, but after my own bus crash I felt a rant coming on. I thought the driver and his apprentice were treating their passengers like animals and with no respect. I was almost ready to stand up and waggle my finger, but realised it would probably not help and could prolong the experience. So, like the rest of the passengers, I sat back and accepted that this was the way things work here.

Then I reached the Senegal border and sat waiting for some form of public transport to Abene, but that didn't look likely and darkness was falling. So, I decided to take a motorcycle taxi. Halfway home, the driver hit a sandbank on the mud track a little too enthusiastically. We skidded from side to side before both of us nosedived across the handlebars. Thankfully the sand was soft, and bar a graze and a twisted ankle, we were fine.

Khady had also returned from a trip to her mother's village and told me she'd brought a gift. It was the horn of a goat. We buried it, in a small ceremony, at the centre of our land where it will protect our home from evil spirits. Although we in the West may laugh at such superstitions, they're often derived from advice handed down over generations. Back in the day, Diola villages along the River Casamance were ripe picking for slave traders. Even now, the collective consciousness is fresh with memories of friends and family mysteriously disappearing in the night, never to be seen again, so a goat's horn for protection seems like a good idea.

Christmas was fast approaching but unlike in England, where there was tinsel overload and a perpetual shopping frenzy, here you'd barely know it. Although there is a small Christian community in Abene that will celebrate the holiday, for the vast majority of the population it'll be just another day and in answer to the popular song, no, many don't know it's Christmas time.

On Christmas Eve, I was visited by three wise Rastas bearing wine, whiskey and beer. That was the end of that day. As a Christmas present, I bought myself a *djembe* and started lessons with my friend Bunja Camara. Most people come to Abene specifically to learn to play this drum, whereas I'd managed to spend two years here without touching one.

Christmas Day itself was dreadful. It wasn't my first terrible Christmas abroad – I've had joyful festive seasons on the beach in Sydney and in the heart of Bangkok but have also been trapped on a remote Ugandan lake island with a group of Alabamian fundamentalist missionaries and in Hanoi with nothing but a six-pack of Tiger beer, a tube of Pringles and a "family edited" version of a Pamela Anderson movie.

On this particular occasion, a fellow that both Khady and I had trusted deceived us. We'd just offered him a job looking after our land and to guard the place whilst we were away. I'll call him "Derrière".

Derrière stole money from us – an amount that goes a very long way here. Khady had known him for years, he had a wife and baby in the village and a life in Abene. Since this incident he has not been able to return and is now separated. Although it was a relatively large amount, I wouldn't have thought it big enough to risk losing everything, especially given that we'd just offered him a decent job with a good wage.

I entrusted Derrière with the cash to buy something. He disappeared and didn't return. We gave him the benefit of the doubt for a day or two. It was Christmas morning when I realised he'd scammed us. His wife arrived in tears. So we went to his home town of Bignona and found him at his mother's house. Obviously young Derrière is not the sharpest tool in the box, heading for his family house in a dusty junction town. He greeted me with a smile and attempted a handshake. When we asked what had happened, he sat smiling and then whistled a jolly tune. You can imagine how well that went over. His brother said he'd spent all the money on women and booze. Meanwhile, I didn't have any cash coming in for another month and was wondering how I was going to feed my family.

His family are related to Khady's and they begged us tearfully to give them a chance. "Wait two days and we'll return the money in full." They had a son in France who'd send it via Western Union. I agreed and went home. Two days came and went and we were fed more excuses. Khady told me she wanted Derrière put in prison, but couldn't be seen by the family to wish that. It had to come from me. A few of Khady's friends told her that he'd stolen from others before and always got away with it.

"So why didn't you tell us when you knew he was coming to our house?" she asked to vacant shrugs.

I needed to show to the village that I'm not a soft touch, once news had spread about the incident. I was trying to figure out the justice system. It seemed that if we reported this, Derrière would be jailed until the money was repaid. I strongly suspected he still had the money and we'd heard a rumour he was going to use it to buy a motorbike. So, we went to the police in Bignona. I sat in front of the chief of police, a large man with a tremendous walrus moustache, who made me feel like a silly little boy when I said I'd trusted someone with my money.

"This is Africa!"

I was beginning to hate that phrase.

"Don't worry," he told me. "He'll pay." He gave me a shifty smile and his moustache twitched. I knew I was in safe hands.

I was given a police summons and we went off to Derrière's house where he was sitting, drinking tea and looking smug. When I handed him the paper, the grin was wiped from his face and for the first time he'd looked scared. Yes, I'm an easy-going friendly guy who likes to think the best of people. Derrière had obviously seen that as a sign of weakness and, along with the family connection which he thought would make us more lenient, decided it could be exploited. Big mistake. He pleaded with Khady as I strode back to Kermit.

Derrière was required to be at the police station at 3pm. We arrived, chatted with the gendarmes and when the chief arrived, Derrière was called in.

At this point I was thinking that this is my word against his. I had no evidence. Perhaps he'd come up with some excuse. But no, the police just automatically believed me. Given the fact he was guilty, I was happy about this, but I realised I could accuse anybody of anything. On this occasion, the system worked for me, but there could be, and probably are, some horrendous miscarriages of justice.

Derrière gave some excuse but the police just laughed. Every time he looked up, they told him to lower his eyes; he was not worthy. They sent him out back and ordered him to strip, then called him back in. He walked back in, holding his hands to cover himself and looking thoroughly humiliated. I almost started feeling sorry for him and wondered if I could live with myself, thinking of him locked up in what I presume are horrible conditions for the sake of some cash. His older brother was there and pleaded us to be lenient. The police advised me to demand return of all the money and only then would he be released from jail.

This was Friday afternoon. We were back home on Saturday morning when the police rang us to say the family had delivered the cash in full. Derrière has never returned to Abene as his former friends and family, who call Khady their sister, will beat him up. His wife thanked me and said he needed to be taught a lesson. A few months later we heard that he had stolen from somebody else.

Shortly after, we had a problem with the jakarta driver that Khady employed. I'd purchased the jakarta – a cheap Chinese motorbike that local youth drive as a taxi service – in order for Khady to run a small business. It was Khady's cousin, so she was upset and sad, but insisted on going to the police. This is very unusual here, as people usually don't when it's family. He's obviously not the brightest of sparks, as his sister is the wife of Derrière, so he must have realised we weren't going to give him a pat on the back and say everything was fine.

Finding a new driver was a frustrating experience. Several people failed to show up after promising to do so. I thought people were desperate for jobs.

"No," Khady said. "They're desperate for money."

Then she went to sprinkle some water on the bike that a marabout had blessed, whilst I sat smirking. Within an hour a good friend called to say he had the perfect driver for us, who showed up the same day.

December and January are the busiest months for tourists, meaning there are two or three more than normal. Plenty of Gambian "bumsters" arrive. These are young guys who hang around in tourist areas of Gambia, providing "services" to tourists. They all cross the border to Abene for the annual festival that takes place between Christmas and New Year. It was a little frustrating when they'd continually offer to guide me and show me around, when I was the resident and they the visitor. Besides hassling me, they are generally on the prowl for European women. It's not surprising so many come, as they seem to be fairly successful at this.

One day as I strolled along the beach, a jolly young bumster approached me, dancing.

"Hello, what is your good name? I am Dancer."

"My nice name is walker," I replied.

"And your country ... ah, my colonial master. So, are you from Dartmoor or London?"

In a land of random conversations, that was random.

Abene Festivalo is one of the annual highlights in Abene. It's a cultural showcase for musicians from the Casamance, from across Senegal, neighbouring countries and occasionally, Senegalese musicians living overseas.

I went with Khady, Bassirou and a brother or cousin, Adama. A power cut had delayed the 9pm kick off, so it was even darker than usual as we approached down the sandy tracks. Crowds of young people waited outside the stage area, to hang out and listen, unable to afford the 500 CFA (75p) entrance fee. Older women had set up makeshift stalls selling café *touba*, omelettes, biscuits and so on.

We entered and sat near the sandy stage. Too close as it happens, as the sound was ear-splittingly loud. For the first hour or so, rappers stalked the stage, trousers half mast in the gangsta rap style and their sidekicks spraying fire into the crowd from spray cans. Again the health and safety manager was absent. Kids from the crowd would run on stage. Some, dissolving in a fit of giggles and running back, others thrusting some coins or perhaps a hat into the hands of the musicians. Adama suddenly appeared on stage, shouting political slogans whilst a *kora* player tinkled. I wasn't entirely sure what he was saying, but everyone cheered wildly. As he roused the crowd to a frenzy the *kora* player started swirling the instrument around his head and playing it upside down, like an African *griot* Hendrix.

Afterwards, there was a succession of *djembe* groups, each better than the last. After a drumming intro, women would sing in a high-pitched wail and then suddenly appear, taking the stage to dance. I never cease to be amazed by the craziness of the dancing styles, which Khady, a dancer herself, has promised to teach me. Occasionally the official dancers would step back and members of the audience would come forth, each trying to outdo the other. *Djembe* orchestras, reggae bands, stilt dancers, lion men, clowns, knife cutters and contortionists – each performance more spectacular than the one before.

The contortionist formed a human belt around one of the dancers. I want one and think they'll be all the rage on Parisian catwalks this time next year. The knife cutter worked himself into a frenzy before slashing at his arms with a knife, stabbing at himself and ripping the knife out of his mouth as if to tear open his cheek. It was only when zooming in on the photographs that I saw he was slicing with the blunt edge of the knife. Khady was aghast at his trickery, but said most knife cutters have magical powers, due to their gris-gris and mystical potions. She often tells me her father's party trick was to cut open his abdomen, pull out his guts and then stuff them back in. Now, that'd be a show-stopper.

Knowing how tranquil Abene is for the rest of the year, it is an extraordinary week for me, perhaps akin to how farmers and villagers in Glastonbury must feel. Whereas normally you can count the number of tourists on a hand with some missing fingers, during this week all the hotels fill, restaurants and pop-up restaurants bustle, the beaches thrive and there is generally a great vibe with tourists across the world, all mad for African music and culture.

I was lucky that as the official photographer, I had front row seats for every event. Each evening, Khady, Gulliver and I would wander along to the village centre take our positions, greet the many villagers we know and enjoy a perfect view. Khady even took to the stage a couple of times to dance to the music.

After the disappointment of Christmas Day itself, I wondered about New Year's Eve and whether again that would be another damp squib. I needn't have worried as it turned out to be one of the best I have ever experienced. That is something coming from someone who celebrated Hogmanay with Gary Glitter in Edinburgh (before his downfall, I hasten to add); at Apocalypse Now nightclub in Hanoi; and awesome street parties in Sydney.

Following further performances, we walked down to the beach where one of the hotels hosts the annual New Year's Eve celebration. A DJ played Senegalese pop and there were perhaps a thousand or more people there including just about everybody I knew from the village, overseas Senegalese who'd returned home and all the toubabs. We sat around a large bonfire on the beach under the African sky with paper lanterns floating upwards. Then various *Wolof sabar* drum groups thrashed away in candle-lit coconut groves whilst we tucked into freshly grilled prawns and ice-cold beers. It was sublime.

THE CASAMANCE

A fire glows in the darkness, drums beat, dancers contort to impossible rhythms. Two white men gyrate, looking like a pair of drunken uncles at a wedding. That would be myself and Shaun, an old school friend. We are in my garden in Abene and Wakily, one of the best drum and dance groups in the Casamance, if not all of Senegal, are performing. Just another evening at the Little Baobab.

Abruptly, the drumming stops. I watch as a local lad whispers urgently to Khady and Saly, Wakily's leader. Khady stamps out the fire and the group makes to leave.

"Go to bed, be quiet," Khady whispers to me softly. "The rebels are coming."

By a curious fate of geography and arbitrary lines drawn on maps by the previous colonial rulers, the Casamance is separated from the rest of Senegal by the Gambia, a 400 mile or so finger-like projection, with a width of often only 20 miles to either side of the river after which it is named. The Casamance is known as the breadbasket of Senegal, being a fertile green region compared to the Sahel of the North. The Casamancais became increasingly frustrated at their resources being plundered by the North whilst little effort was placed on development of the region. Consequently, there has been a separatist movement in the Casamance since the early 1980s, with some of its residents fighting a low-level guerrilla war.

One night, in February 2013, three people were killed during an attack in nearby Kafountine. Until this point, the only effect of the rebel activity in the Casamance on my own life had been the inconvenience of military blockades en route to local towns, and the closure of roads at night. Scuffles are sporadic and rare, almost never involving foreigners; the last incident was in the mid-1990s. Frustratingly, the British Foreign Office still advises against most travel in the Casamance, whilst other nations have deemed it perfectly safe. For example, most tourists here are elderly retired French couples, hardly your typical war-zone junkies.

Following the disbandment of Wakily's performance we heard nothing, but on a walk through Abene the next morning, we saw a merchant rebuilding a wall of his shop. The bandits had blasted a hole in it and robbed him. This is a local African guy. A young man with a wife and child, just scraping a living.

For the next week or so I heard many rumours. A crazy French man in Kafountine had played Russian roulette and killed himself (apparently true); someone was shot driving through a roadblock without stopping (not sure); rebels had robbed the bank in nearby Kafountine before coming to Abene (true; the bank safe lay opened and abandoned in the road for months).

Everyone says the rebels are mostly just opportunistic bandits and consequently, for me, this is a blip that doesn't particularly worry me, besides feeling for the people directly affected. Abene is a community where everyone knows each other and any crime I've heard of has been opportunistic rather than malicious. The previous year had seen higher numbers of visitors than ever coming to the festival and it would be a great shame, culturally and for the local population, if tourism was affected by incidents like these. Hopefully, the truth will come out and be reported for everyone's peace of mind. Locals are sure that the negative media coverage is perpetrated by Dakar or the Gambia to hinder development and slow tourism in order to maintain their own interests.

Quite frankly, you've more chance of being robbed on a trip to London, but it seems to me that there is always heightened fear and paranoia where Africa is concerned. It never seems to take long for the "dark continent" narrative to reemerge whenever there's a crisis, as the recent Ebola outbreak proves. A holiday-maker was beheaded recently in the Canary Islands, but tourists still flock there. Had that happened in an African nation I'm sure that tourism would be decimated.

The rebel forces are known as the Movement of Democratic Forces of the Casamance (MFDC) and they first declared independence for the Casamance in 1947. Not all Diola's are separatists but almost all separatists are Diola. The Diola's were notoriously resistant to colonisation – first by the Portuguese and subsequently by the French – and it's not surprising that more recently they have been resistant to rule from Dakar. The conflict has run for more than 30 years, the longest in contemporary Africa.

The MFDC have been fighting the Senegalese army since 1982, resulting in the death of thousands, many civilian, and the displacement of tens of thousands of people. The conflict has spilled over to involve neighbouring Guinea Bissau and the Gambia, leading to banditry along the borders and an increase in the smuggling of both legal and illegal products.

The conflict has avoided the child soldiers and mass amputations of other more recent West African wars, although atrocities have happened. The Senegalese army do not take, or keep, prisoners in battle and there have been civilian massacres. The reverse is also true and the rebels have been reported to rape civilians. Khady herself was held hostage as a young girl, but escaped unharmed.

There have been many attempts at negotiating a peace agreement, but as yet to no avail. Since the 1990s, the MFDC has been plagued by internal conflict. When President Wade was elected in 2000, he brought some simple ideas: no intermediaries (he excluded the Gambia and Guinea Bissau from the peace process), no assistance to any MFDC faction and direct talks with the real separatists.

Although the Senegalese army was much improved and better behaved, there were no significant results. In 2002, the *Joola* – a ship that ran between Dakar and Ziguinchor – sank, resulting in the death of 2,000 people including

Khady's cousin; a direct result of mismanagement of the *Joola* by the state.

Wade tried to establish direct contact with the rebels by way of community organisations and religious leaders. He poured money into and improved conditions in the Casamance. He strengthened ties with both Gambia and Guinea Bissau, brought refugees home and offered MFDC fighters exit strategies.

Senegal has deployed several thousand troops to combat thinly spread guerrilla units, which have the advantage of fighting on home ground. On the other hand, the MFDC lacks both the firepower to drive out the army and the support of the majority of Casamance people.

As with many African conflicts, fighters derive benefit from war economy, so have little inclination to stop despite increasingly vague reasons for the initial conflict. There are few local resources for rebels, beyond cannabis farms and robbing local people. There are now people who have tied their entire lives to the conflict, hence they can't easily abandon it. Many of the rebel leaders started fighting as teenagers 30 years ago, with bow and arrows, sticks and stones.

One important factor in the lack of common ground is the Diola strength of identity, as well as Senegalese pride. Senegal has long considered itself special within Africa – more advanced and more developed – making it hard for them to consider Casamance as a separate entity.

On the ground, I've seen little evidence of popular support for the rebel activity. The general public is tired and wants the region to develop. In the 1970s, the Casamance was an up-and-coming tourist destination and it remains a perfect region to develop community eco-tourism. Macky Sall, the recently elected president, vowed to sort out the situation and peace agreements have now take place in Europe. The local people with whom I've discussed it are fed up with the conflict and just want to get on with their lives.

PALM WINE DRUNKARDS

It is pitch black; the nearest source of electricity is 20 miles away. A tribal rhythm fills the air – manic drumming and the clang, boom and steam of dozens of women smashing wood and metal in a frenzied beat, singing their hearts out in a high-pitched cacophony.

The women form a circle into which shadowy figures dance. It is dimly lit by a fire. One young woman, a whirling dervish, spins and spins uncontrollably, seemingly in a trance. The beat quickens, the woman's eyes widen and everyone stomps their feet, kicking up the dust. Faster and faster she spins, before collapsing in a heap. Older women carry her away, shaking, drooling, limbs twitching.

It's tragic that the Casamance has had such a troubled history; by rights, it should be up with southeast Asia and India on the world's great travellers' trails. The region is full of lush tropical landscapes, friendly people, great food, culture and some of the best music and dance of the continent. It's the closest tropical zone to Europe, being only a six-hour flight from London. Yet, due to the recent conflict, besides a few French retirees, it's almost devoid of tourists.

I often take off for a ramble, and had decided to visit the nearby Karoninke Islands in the mangrove swamps to the south of Kafountine. The Karoninka are a sub-tribe of the Diola who speak their own dialect and have been converted to Christianity by Dutch missionaries. Before any trip, there are certain Diola traditions we must adhere to. First I have to make sure I'm wearing all of my gris-gris, especially the one Ibrahima, the *Baye Fall* guy, gave me on my first visit to Dakar. Even my camera bag has various talismanic seeds in it, placed there by Khady. Then before I go, she'll sprinkle water across the gate, to give me good luck.

Getting a boat to the islands can test one's patience. I'd tried in vain this time to find out about timings, but despite boats leaving every day, nobody could tell me when. I'm often exasperated trying to find out the simplest of information here. In Africa, traditionally a person will be told what they need to know by the person, usually an elder, who is authorised to tell them. What they don't need to know, they needn't think about; it doesn't concern them. It's bad to ask too many questions and not knowing can be essential for existence: there are some things you shouldn't know and which could bring harm on yourself or on the person who told you.

Which is all very well, but sometimes I just want to know what time the boat is leaving.

After several hours under a straw shack, waiting and swatting flies, a large dug-out canoe arrived. Masses of people, containers of palm wine and other luggage, including a very large trussed-up pig, were loaded on board. Something was wrong with the boat, so we all waded off and on to another boat. That one leaked, so, with damp trousers, we changed boats again. Eventually we left, except the driver had clearly never driven a boat before. He crashed three times, once knocking a passenger into the river as we hit a mangrove branch. The other passengers were angry and it was getting late. I'd left Abene at 10am, it was 5pm and I'd only travelled a few miles down the road, a familiar African travel story.

Still, once this was behind me it was beautiful, with plentiful birdlife, scenic mangrove swamps and glimpses of remote sandy, palm-tree lined beaches. As always I felt privileged to have this on my doorstep. Once we landed I started walking through giant corridors of baobab trees towards the village of Kouba, my destination. I had a contact there, a local Karoninka tribesman called Christophe. (Most people on the islands have been baptised with European names). The dialect is different to the Diola I speak, for example instead of "*kassumei kep*" (hello), everyone says, "*kassumei lama*". Other phrases were less alike.

I asked after Christophe but he'd gone to Ziguinchor and would be back in the morning. His grandmother, Bernadette, was there though, out tending the marijuana fields. Ah yes, that's the thing about these islands, they're full of these plantations, stretching miles as far as the eye can see like prairie wheat fields in the American Midwest, sort of. I was intrigued and asked about the market, but they were understandably a little coy. It seems that although illegal, the authorities turn a blind eye. After all, the police don't have a boat, they have to take the public ferry and then cross 10 miles of island, so they can hardly turn up unannounced. For the locals, it is a crop, simple as that. They could grow onions or tomatoes, but marijuana pays more so they grow that. I wandered down to find Bernadette, a sweet little old woman, with her grandchildren, all preteen, watering their herbs.

Although it seemed a little amusing to watch old women and kids tending to miles and miles of marijuana fields, there is a dark side to drugs in West Africa. Given the conflict, the remoteness and general lawlessness, as well as the proximity to Africa's biggest narco-state, Guinea Bissau, it's not too surprising that the marijuana fields are here and so easily accessible. Much of Europe's cocaine is trafficked through nearby Guinea Bissau, and indeed, the biggest hotel in Abene was closed down as it was a front for this trade. If anyone has a spare £650,000 it's advertised online for sale. Not too bad for a 20-bedroom hotel with manicured lawns, staff and a private runway.

Approaching the river, I met a local man, Felix, and he told me to go ahead and borrow his canoe. People here were some of the friendliest I'd met in Senegal with no demands for money prevalent elsewhere. I launched and paddled out into the stream which was flowing quite fast as the tide was rising up the saltwater estuary. It was very wobbly and not for the first time I questioned the wisdom of hauling around expensive camera gear. I made it and pulled up at a little island around the bend in the river. Swarms of birds flew away and crabs scuttled as I pulled up and walked onto the beach.

A group of men sat under a small shelter, wearing shorts and merrily bantering after clearly consuming their fair share of palm wine, known locally as *bounok*.

"Come, come" they invited me and I sat down amongst the piles of shucked oyster shells. One of the men turned out to be a professor of linguistics from Dakar University. He'd returned to his home village for the holiday period and had spent the day catching giant capitaine fish, eating oysters, downing *bounok* and swimming. He looked content. Before I knew it, Eduardo, my new best friend, nipped off and returned with an old plastic oil drum filled with fresh *bounok*. He swept a layer of scum and floating bees off the top and glugged it into coconut-shell glasses.

I'd previously tried palm wine and found it to be an acquired taste, resembling the liquid that runs off of set yoghurts that has turned rancid. I sort of like it but too much makes me queasy. I had clearly never tried fresh *bounok* before. This was a revelation, a sweet alco-pop, and one of the finest natural juices I've ever tried. I couldn't get enough. I have palm trees at the Little Baobab and Eduardo said he'd come and help me tap them. A glass of this in the morning, before the sugar turns to alcohol will be just the ticket.

Bellies full and with a mild buzz, I settled back into the canoe and drifted back as pelicans and herons roosted and the sun began to set. I was hot and dived into the crystal-clear waters. The sky turned orange and the sun shimmered, appearing twice its normal size. In case I'd forgotten I was in Africa, a distant drumbeat began. It was one of those beautiful, sublime moments.

I returned and Christophes' house was empty, so I went with Eduardo and joined a group of guys drinking more *bounok*, this time of the rancid-yoghurt variety, then tucked into a platter of rice and river fish. As I was finishing, Bernadette, the Grandma, arrived and said dinner was ready. Not wanting to offend, I went for my second dinner, which was "meat". As I ate, I enquired what the meat was – it's usually goat, but this tasted more like venison.

"Monkey." I wasn't too thrilled by this answer but at that point I had nearly finished eating.

I then headed into the village centre, the source of the drumbeat and where a traditional wedding ceremony was occurring.

"It's no problem to come?" I asked.

"No, no, it'll be an honour for them to have a toubab here."

One girl was dancing hard and fell into some kind of trance. She was wearing a T-shirt emblazoned with the words "Sex Instructor"[8]. If I didn't know better (women don't drink or smoke and this is a traditional society), I'd have thought she

---

[8]Most clothes sold in the markets are secondhand ones from the West. As many people here are illiterate they often have no idea what they're displaying, in the same way I didn't when I wore a T-shirt covered with Chinese symbols. For all I knew I could have been advertising potatoes.

was on drugs. One minute she was dancing ecstatically and the next minute she was bug-eyed, shaking. Elder women rushed in to grip her tightly and lower her to the ground, where she lay twitching.

The beat picked up again and an old man passed me a filthy calabash filled with sweet palm wine, which I drank before starting my own funky strut into the circle's centre. Like anything in life, once you start, you have to commit and continue. You also have to time it right. Start too far back, like I did, and you're strutting on your own in the dark, not sure if anyone can see you. I felt like a right pillock, but had to carry on. Eventually I emerged into the firelight. Everyone cheered. I swivelled and moonwalked my way back into the shadows, high-fiving my new best friends.

The next morning I had planned to take a trip back into the swamp. But I started itching and realised I was crawling with tiny black insects. At first I thought it was fleas but it was *mutu mutu* – a tiny biting insect that causes an intense fiery itch for a few minutes. If you can resist scratching, the itch soon fades. By the time the sun rose, they had disappeared.

Another problem was the number of pigs which foraged around the island. They carry a parasite that buries itself into your feet and eats you from inside. This is not as bad as it sounds and at worst you'd just have to lop off a toe or two. I found two itchy black dots, one on my heel and one on a toe. Upon my return, Khady took a needle and from each hooked out a small wriggling maggot. I hoped they hadn't laid eggs.

Christophe's son, Sadio, said he'd come with me and I launched back into the dug-out and back to the small island where I'd drunk the *bounok*. I met Augustine, an old man with one of the best jobs in the world. Everyday he canoes to the island and sits under a palm tree, drinking *bounok* and making funnels out of palm leaves. These are then inserted into holes tapped in the trees and the sap flows through into bottles to form wine.

I canoed around the island onto an even bigger island, crossed salt pans on foot, sending thousands of crabs scuttling to either side of me and emerged at an idyllic white sand beach next to a wide river. It was too late in the morning to see the monkeys and antelope that locals hunt, but I saw their tracks.

Very, very hot, I slipped into the clear, cool waters and swam out a few hundred metres. As I gave my finest Freddie Mercury "deh oh!" my voice echoed around as if I was at the bottom of a canyon. Had I seen a vine and brought my loincloth, you may never have heard from me again.

I couldn't get enough of the tranquility, so bid farewell to Sadio, who paddled back, leaving me like Robinson Crusoe on my own private desert island. I've always enjoyed time by myself.

Once the soft lapping of the canoe paddle faded from earshot and Sadio turned around a bend in the river, it was me, the birds and a few antelope. At least, I hoped that was all. I mooched around, built a little shelter from palm leaves, gathered firewood, cooled off with swims and sipped from an old dusty oil can filled with five litres of *bounok* that Sadio had left with me. I was in my element.

As darkness drew in, the remoteness struck me. There's no light pollution and the stars were as magnificent as any I've seen, including in the deserts of five continents. The fire kept the darkness at bay, there were the usual creaks and groans of the cooling ground and scuffling of small animals, but nothing that overtly worried me. Unlike the plains of Eastern and Southern Africa, besides snakes, there's not too much that can harm you here. Having said that, I did hear about a German guy on a trans-African cycling trip. Camping remotely in the Gambian interior, his spectacles were the only item found after hyenas paid a visit.

I lay under the shelter, listening to the night noises, before drifting into a deep sleep born of exercise, fresh air, too much sunshine and not a little sweet *bounok*.

The next morning was magnificent. I was up before dawn, and watched as the orange sun slowly rose into the clear blue skies above the vivid-green tropical forest. Parrots fluttered in the trees. Just as I was thinking I never wanted to leave, Sadio appeared and we paddled back. As I waded to the shore up to my thighs in river water, I enquired about crocodiles.

"Ah *oui, beaucoup* crocodiles," came the slightly worrying response. I think he was joking.

I journeyed back on Christophe's bicycle, cycling across shimmering salt pans and carrying it by hand in the dug-out canoe that took me back to the mainland. At this time of year it gets quite windy with the *harmatten* blowing dust down from the Sahara. I battled the wind the entire journey home and by the time I arrived into Abene I could barely walk after getting off the bike. The sun was setting and I saw a vision approaching: a slender African woman in flowing gown and with a huge pot elegantly balanced on her head. As I got closer, I realised it was Khady and felt overjoyed to be alive.

THE TREE OF LIFE

The Baobab tree provides shelter, clothing, food and water for both animals and humans. In many villages the baobab tree is a centre for community life. Meetings take place under its broad branches, and in some places it is the source of religious beliefs and rites. Senegal has selected the baobab to be its national symbol. Some say that if you drink water in which a baobab's seeds have been soaked, you will be safe from a crocodile attack.

After months of working hard, suffering the extreme climate and being the only Brit in the village, I looked forward to some visitors. It would be great to have a normal conversation and for people to see what we'd achieved. Was I heading in the right direction? Could I entertain people and would it be up to the standards they'd demand? I invited my family and aside from the joy of spending time together, they would also act as a trial run for when we opened our guest house to paying visitors. It was my mother and father's first trip to Africa proper, their first to meet Khady, and their first to meet their first grandson, Gulliver.

I wanted it to be right and aimed to impress, showing them I hadn't gone crazy, had a good and comfortable lifestyle and to help them understand the bigger picture of what I was trying to achieve. As usual, Africa ganged up on me, making this trickier than I expected.

The first setback was when it became apparent the ground wasn't going to dry out and we couldn't finish the toilet and shower in time. Khady and I were determined they'd stay with us and not in a hotel, so we built a temporary jungle bathroom, complete with (bucket) flushing loo and a prawn-shell decorated shower.

Kermit had been very reliable over the months, but chose the morning of their arrival for several problems in the steering to manifest. I raced to the garage and they worked fast, but we were cutting it fine to arrive at the airport on time. As the mechanics finished, someone parked in front of me and disappeared, leaving me sitting helplessly in the sun for 10 minutes. Don't you love those moments?

Finally, we arrived at the airport. We were on time but Fenton's rule of travel came true: transport will always arrive late, unless you yourself are running late, whereupon it will arrive early. The plane had landed 45 minutes ahead of time and my parents were standing looking hot and worried, surrounded by touts. After a hug, I took them to safety and explained the set up:

"This is Africa and everything has gone wrong."

Kermit wasn't quite hopping in a healthy manner. There were some worrying grating sounds. The airport mechanic came to help and told me that the ball-bearings had gone on the front left wheel. The previous mechanic hadn't seen that. So, we drove down to Brikama, the nearest town, and saw a helpful-looking man who of course knew a man who could fix anything. That's the great thing about this part of the world, there's always a fixer around. He jumped in the back with Mum and Dad and off we went.

This was a serious introduction to Africa for parents. We drove for about five miles down bumpy pothole-ridden dust tracks, through forests, deeper and deeper into the bush. Just a bit further, the fixer kept saying and I could see the folks were anxious wondering if we were being lead into an ambush. Of course, this sort of thing happens to me all the time and Khady was speaking in the Diola language and knows exactly who she can trust. Finally, we arrived at a small house in the middle of nowhere, where the mechanic just happened to have exactly the right materials. We were all given chairs and sat catching up, whilst chickens clucked around and curious kids curtseyed to us and asked us our names. Welcome to Africa!

Two hours, £10 down and with Kermit sounding much healthier, we set off towards the border, reaching it as darkness fell. We passed a ceremonial procession with *Simba*, the lion dancer, who jumped on the side of the car and hissed through the window at my mother. The Senegalese border was closed, so we continued as illegal aliens until we reached the first town, where the military had decided to close the road and said we'd have to sleep there. Now this wasn't what I had in mind for Mum and Dad's first night.

Khady spoke to the soldier and after some negotiations he let us sneak past, down a side road. We were on our way again.

The Senegalese say that when you have your own land and house, your life can be tranquil. Fatou, Khady's sister had prepared the house and a huge platter of fire-grilled fish, rice, salad and a strong mustard and onion marinade. I had a few bottles of Julbrew, Gambia's finest, chilling in my cooler along with a bottle of lady petrol (rosé). We gathered around and ate in the communal African style, listening to the jungle noises beneath the night sky.

The next day, I was able to show them around properly. We have a shaded jungle glade where we set up our table and chairs and relaxed for the morning. Although my parents have been to many parts of the world including India and southeast Asia, they said this was without doubt the hottest place they'd ever been (and it had cooled slightly compared to the previous months).

Khady and friends had some surprises. Jumbo's dad, Bakary – the chap who'd been helping me with much of the clearing, fencing and roofing – arrived leading a goat. This was introduced to us before being led round the back for dispatch. For the next couple of days we grilled it, stewed it and ate it. Babies Simon and Khady were brought round for inspection and then in the late afternoon, we heard drumming and chanting. A procession entered our land including a *Koumpo* and *Gomala*, a masked gorilla-like dancer. Everyone sang and danced and obviously Mum and Dad got dragged up to have a go. Palm wine appeared, more goat was cooked and as I watched Dad playing with the children, Mum all wrapped up in Gulliver and Khady dancing, the troubles of the previous day were forgotten.

For the next few days, we explored the village and met everyone, relaxed on the empty beaches, visited markets, walked to the nearest town and took a boat trip in the nearby mangroves, viewing an island with hundreds of pelicans. For a couple of afternoons, Dad even helped me clear some jungle. Although my life might not be for them, they could see I was in my element and they felt much happier.

The final evening in Abene was one of the special moments. Dad and I had returned from a successful search for a beer. As we walked up the driveway, we heard the soft bubbling sounds of the *kora*, the West African harp. My friend Bunja, a percussionist, and Hami, a *griot kora* player from Gambia, had turned up. They played all night and sang songs to Gulliver, my parents, Khady and me.

The next day we were leaving for Khady's mother's village before continuing to the Gambia. There was a little snap, crackle and pop upon departure: we found a highly venomous puff adder, which before we knew what was happening, Bakary killed. Having watched the adventurer Bear Grylls on television, I knew exactly what to do and lopped off the head with my machete, then buried it before the kids or the dog started playing with it. Snakes can retain poison for 24 hours or so.

We then drove down the bush tracks to visit Khady's mother and family. My father and I walked around the village and as most people know me there by now they shouted out greetings. We returned for some beef stew before carrying along the bush tracks into the Gambia. The Customs man stamped us in, no questions asked and it was as if we'd never been to Senegal. Then after an hour of bumpy dirt tracks we hit the main road and the bright lights of the beach resorts.

Upon arrival on the Smiling Coast, instead of our usual hotel, Mum and Dad treated us to somewhere a little nicer and so we went to the Leybato Hotel on the beach in Fajara. You couldn't fault the setting: a terrace overlooking golden sands and straw-roofed huts amidst a tropical garden. There were plenty of other things you could fault though. The place where Khady and I usually stay may only cost a fiver and be slightly down at heel, but they are very friendly and always fix any problem quickly.

Besides lying on a beach, we took a stroll in Bijilo forest, a small pocket of forest that is home to hundreds of vervet monkeys and the shyer red colobus. Later we visited the sacred crocodile pools (where women bathe in the waters if they are having fertility problems). Dad had obviously relaxed into the African spirit. Last time I was in the UK, I had showed a photograph of me with a croc and he'd looked at me as if I was a nutter. Here, I spotted him standing surrounded by four crocodiles concentrating on taking a picture of a bird.

On the final day, we had lunch under a thatched roof next to a lagoon filled with crocodiles. About 10 metres behind, with no fence in between, lay tourists slowly turning red on the beach, oblivious. I started to think a little health and safety legislation may not be such a bad thing. We dropped Mum and Dad at the airport and returned to our hotel feeling a little lonely.

We had several visitors after that, but perhaps the most impressive has been Tony, who was on a solo journey through Morocco, Mauritania, Senegal, Gambia, Guinea, Guinea Bissau and Mali. Tony is blind, 80 percent deaf and had recently had a kidney transplant. He's also published his own travel book; we were introduced when his publisher asked me to interview him via Skype. After the interview, I joked that maybe I'd meet him in Senegal. You don't make jokes like that to Tony, who's travelled to 66 countries in all seven continents. Six months or so later, I received an email telling me he was on his way.

We arranged to meet in Bignona, 50 miles from Abene and he thought he'd be there about lunchtime. Late afternoon, a Gambian guy called me saying he'd just dropped Tony at the border with Senegal and he should be there soon. Tony had no mobile phone, so he was now travelling blind, so to speak.

Darkness fell and I was waiting on the side of a busy road.

"Just look for the guy with the stick," Tony had laughed on the phone earlier. By about 9pm I was getting worried. I knew that roads are often closed by the military in this region and figured he was probably having to sleep on the roadside, like I had done the previous year. Just as I was about to give up, he arrived, totally unfazed by the situation.

One of his questions to me when he was researching this trip was "what are the people like and will they rip me off?" I replied that like anywhere, most people are decent, honest and hard working, but there's always the odd rascal. And aside from the official who charged him for a visa that should have been free; someone who took some money whilst helping him with a bank machine; and the border guard who would only let him pass in exchange for his stick, this was true.

We made our way to Khady's uncle's house and entered the compound, which was filled with kids who were surprised to see a couple of toubabs turning up. After a night listening to Tony snore (he always turns his hearing aids off and sleeps well) we awoke and drove to Abene where we spent days walking and getting plenty of stares (not a problem for Tony). Tony is a drummer and so naturally wanted to try *djembe* drums as well as other percussion such as the talking drum and *bongo* (a Guinean instrument made from calabash with hacksaw blades to pluck, making a twanging noise). He'd unselfconsciously dance to any music and uncharacteristically, I found myself joining him.

Tony blasted into our lives and briefly lit them before heading off, as travellers are wont to do. The evening before his departure, a friend emailed from Guinea Bissau saying there was a coup and shooting in the capital so Tony should stay away. I made the suggestion he simply reverse his route and go first to Mali, then Guinea and finally Bissau, if safe, before returning to Senegal for his flight home.

Watching Tony head off in a bush taxi filled with strangers and not knowing where he'd be staying that night, I felt emotional. Happy to have made a new friend, slightly worried, but privileged for the time we'd spent together and allowing me to experience the world Tony's way.

In retrospect, I hadn't given the best advice in the world. The day after he left, there was a coup in Bamako, the capital of Mali, all borders were closed and gunfire was reported across the city. Tony was already there, laid low in a hostel following an arduous journey, and waiting for the borders to reopen so he could go to Guinea. I felt terrible, but later he laughed and told me it was he who'd chosen to travel in Africa and nobody could have predicted what was going to happen.

Following our visitors in the early part of the year, Senegal's main tourist season, we were keen to start work on our big house, leaving the current small one that we were living in available for paying guests. It was March and I figured that was plenty of time to finish it before the rains began in July. After all, our small house was built in a little over a month.

I had recently shipped all of my worldly possessions from a storage facility in Sussex to the Little Baobab. I had nowhere to store it all, so had built a makeshift shelter which would be fine in the dry season, but useless in the wet. I hadn't counted on the termites which destroyed some rare antique books.

Once I started unpacking, I regretted not having time to thoroughly sort my belongings before storing and transporting them. I stared at the attachments to a vacuum cleaner I no longer owned; a toaster in a land with no toastable bread; a white satin Elvis jump suit (really) and various electrical goods far too powerful for our solar-powered system. I have an entire library's worth of books which I love, but I'm not sure how long they'll last in a house that sometimes feels alive and a six-month rainy season with 99 percent humidity.

It was amusing to see Khady and her friends' reactions to some of the things.

"What's this?"

"Oh, it's a scraper to get all the mayonnaise out of a jar."

"Why is this book wrapped in plastic?"

"It's an antique, more than 100 years old and worth £100!"

She disappeared laughing, unable to believe this. Mind you, perhaps she was laughing at me for not being organised enough to sell such items that will disintegrate so rapidly here.

After weeks sporting a biro, a tape measure and some scraps of paper I finally designed what would become our family house. The plan was to use the small original one as a guest house and then, depending on how the business developed, build more round houses for more guests as and when we needed them.

Yancoba, the blind builder and his team returned and spent a few weeks making 8000 bricks with sand dug from behind our kitchen. These were left to dry for a couple of weeks and we turned our attention to the foundations.

"You have to be here to supervise" said Khady. "Strange things might happen otherwise."

"Yes, yes" I agreed. But first I had a little paid work in a nearby town that just needed a day or so to finish. I would get that done, then I'd stay home, helping the builders and keeping an eye on things whilst kicking everything to test for strength. A good plan, I decided.

The builders were going to dig the foundations. I thought they were just going to do the main circle of the round house. That's simple, nothing can go wrong. At about 7am, we all stood around muttering and then I launched in, grabbing a spade and showed where I wanted the house. I was told to shut up and crouch down, as I suddenly realised what everyone else was doing. We all raised out hands, someone spoke in Arabic and then we fluttered our hands to the sky. That done, I showed them where to build, helped break the ground and then nipped off to finish my work in Kafountine.

I returned about 6pm. They'd finished digging trenches for the foundations and it looked great. Except for one minor detail: they'd also dug the foundations for the internal walls. The house was now back to front; the front door was at the back and the verandah faced the rear fence. I'd wrongly assumed they understood my arrow facing north on the plan. Oh, bugger.

I quickly thought through the options. Could it work that way round? No, not really as anyone could walk up the path to the house without us knowing. The main view from all points of the land would be the back wall of the house, not the front door and verandah. This is a verandah where I intend to grow old, perhaps in a rocking chair, so I might as well get it right now.

It took me a while to explain. Laying the plans out and orienting it to the correct angle made no sense to anyone but me. They'd spent the entire day breaking their backs under a hot sun and then I swan in and tell them they need to start again. I sent out for some drinks and offered to pay an extra day's labour to alleviate my guilt. Although I couldn't help thinking it was their daft mistake, I should have been there. By this point, we had two months or so to get the roof on before the monsoon season. No problem. A day later, the foundations were correctly aligned.

As I had experienced, in Africa, it is important to watch every detail. Sometimes things seemed to move along fine and I thought, well they've built plenty of houses and with Diannah, have a qualified mason. Then I gave the okay to the positioning of the pipes in the bathroom. After it was all cemented in, I noticed that the waste pipe from the toilet was several feet away from the back wall, meaning it would be positioned out in the middle of the room. I couldn't believe I hadn't noticed that earlier. It's easy to assume certain things are obvious, but the average person in Senegal doesn't have a plumbed-in toilet. Thankfully, it was no problem to shift.

I designed my own kitchen, not that I had much choice. I met a Swiss chap who had just finished a house here, with a thoroughly modern kitchen – work tops, cupboards, the whole shebang.

"Where did you get that?" I enquired, hoping to get my own.

"Ikea." He'd brought it in a shipping container.

We have two kitchens. Outside, there is Khady's African kitchen where we've built a work surface and a place where we can have a barbecue and another space for a charcoal burner that Khady often cooks on. It's raised so she's not squatting or bent double in the traditional manner. This traditional kitchen was something she wanted; it's easy for me to impose my Western ideas when actually she prefers her way. My funky chopping board sits forlornly whilst she continues to chop onions into her hand. The work station is built onto a tiled patio, above which will be a wooden platform, reached by steps, where we can sit level with the tree tops to enjoy the sunset, bird life, or just a cool shady place to relax, perhaps with a glass or two of palm wine.

Inside the house is the "toubab" kitchen where I'll have my gas cooker, fridge and a work surface that curves round with a kind of breakfast bar into the main living room. Somewhere where I can whip up a plate of pasta or a curry when I fancy a change from African food.

Have you ever tried to ask someone to build something like a kitchen when they've absolutely no notion of what you're wittering on about? My builders spent their entire lives being fed from a single pot on a fire. And here's me trying to explain where I want the wine rack. I tried drawing things, but that didn't really work. Diannah stared, turn the paper several times, nodded sagely and clearly hadn't a clue what it meant. If I had any sense, I'd have taken some photographs. Instead, I mucked in and built the damned thing with him, which was in the end far more satisfying.

Work slowed down slightly as the builder Vieux became infected by a devil. English builders can have a reputation for giving implausible excuses, but I can't imagine them trying this one. He raised up a sleeve to show me quite a serious-looking flaky skin condition, like psoriasis. Instantly, everyone declared it was due to a devil and someone's cast an evil spell on him, so he disappeared off into the forest where he would be washed with traditional medicines by the marabout. I tried to ascertain why this was the devil's work and not simply a medical condition.

"It just is. Africa is very dark. There are things you can't understand."

Then Khady told me everyone thinks he will be dead before the end of the rains[9]. Although I don't believe in black magic, I have seen such strange things in my short time here. And I do believe in the powerful effects of belief.

[9]A year or more has passed and Vieux is still alive and kicking.

Bakary helped me make some mud bricks. We dug a hole, tipped in some water and jumped in to stamp around barefoot in the mud. It was a bit like making wine, except instead of a satisfying beverage, we had ourselves some mud. Bunja had a mould and we made 100 bricks. With these we built the chicken house and an oven.

Tierno, the marabout, reappeared after some mysterious travels which Fatou, his wife, knew little about. He made me a fetish to protect the land; a weird crocodile-like creature with metal bottle tops glued all over it with some sticky substance. It seemed the land needs protecting again. I had started feeling a bit down for various reasons. When Khady found some eggs hanging on one of our fence posts, that explained everything. Eggs can have a spell cast on them by a marabout. Someone who wished me to have a problem would then plant them somewhere on my land. Khady said this explained why I wasn't feeling as jaunty as usual.

"Maybe another woman is trying to cause problems and split us up," she mused.

I was really enjoying fatherhood now that Gulliver had begun walking and talking and his little headstrong character emerged. The first few months were hard but it gets easier as time goes on and I crack up every time he stomps around to my music like a traditional Senegalese wrestler.

He's also very inquisitive. One day I saw him pick up something and place it in his mouth. I grabbed him and stuck my finger in his mouth, rummaged around and pulled out a still-twitching frog's head. The rest of the body was nowhere to be seen. It was a white frog, which Khady said was a genie. He's never sick and has a very strong immune system now.

Outdoor playing can't be beaten. As most people of my age will say, when we were kids we'd leave the house in the morning, run around in the fields and woods all day, returning as darkness fell after having gotten up to all sorts of mischief. It seems that's increasingly difficult with people's health and safety fears as well as those of attacks and so on. But these things have always happened – just look at all the pedophilia abuse emerging now from the 1960s and '70s. I can't help thinking that by being paranoid about something that is so rare, despite the image given by today's sensationalist media, the children are losing out on something very special. Happily here in Abene, kids play outside and in the forest. There's barely any traffic and as long as they're wary of snakes, there are no big problems.

African women usually breast feed for at least two years and often longer. Bottles are not much of an option here. The formula isn't good quality and sterilising would be a nightmare. Obviously, this is much easier when you're not going to work. Well, Khady works, but Gulliver's here with her, trying to help.

As a family, we always eat from a communal platter in the local style and Gulliver eats the same as us. I've seen many African children and I've never met a fussy eater here. Maybe we've got that to come, but for now, he happily eats all vegetables, olives and hummus. Maybe he's already realised that if he doesn't eat what he's given, it goes to the dogs and there'll be nothing else.

Babies always sleep in the same bed as their parents in Africa, at least for two or three years. At first I wasn't too keen on this, but now it's fine and I love it. Gulliver sleeps soundly all night and I've only been woken maybe twice in the night since he was born. Khady likes it as she doesn't have to get up to feed him. I know many Westerners are against this, but it works fine for us.

A friend visited me for the first time in three weeks and was flabbergasted at the development of the houses and the gardens. It's true, we don't always notice when we're working day in day out, but we get quite a lot done. Someone once said he is confident no great work of art has ever been created by anyone with excellent internet access[10]. I reckon he's got a point.

Alongside work on the house we built a separate outdoor guest bathroom, a small house for Fakeba, the gardener, and the African kitchen. I continued my various projects as the builders worked on the house. I cleared a path around the

[10] Internet is available at dial-up speeds in Abene, so I don't bother with a connection at home. It's slower than the connection I had in rural Vietnam in 1999.

impenetrable forest. There was much dead bush and prickly stuff that I carefully dragged into strategic piles and burnt.

I hacked a passage through the middle, past a huge termite mound ending up near my morning hammock. When undertaking such work, I'm very careful to only remove dead wood, weeds and the nasty thorny scrub. The main forest remains, but by cleaning, we are providing a more healthy environment for the "good stuff", giving it room to breath and grow, as well as allowing us to enjoy the space.

When I wasn't paying attention, Fakeba, who'd come to help me, set fire to some bush near the fence – I told him to be careful and he said no problem. Then I heard a shout and we all ran, builders included, to fetch buckets of water. A gust of wind had blown the fire onto the fence and it was blazing. Thankfully we extinguished it before much damage was done and the lad, embarrassed, soon had a new section installed. That night there was a guy called "the Fireman" performing in Abene but he wouldn't have been much use because he is a rapper.

We worked on the garden every day and by now were growing pineapple, onions, carrot, beetroot, cabbage, spring onions, chillies, coriander and sunflowers. For the pineapples, we simply twisted the green spiky tops off of the fruit, planted them and they grow. An avocado seed I tossed away has sprouted a tree and Khady's onions grew to the size of tennis balls. We also produced giant guava and several watermelons. One day, I had my palm trees cleaned. I had never realised palms required cleaning, but a palm tree cleaner persuaded me to do it, chopping off all the dead bits so they would flourish, which indeed they did. The leaves were absorbed into the fence.

Then I bought my first cow. A friend of Khady's had a family emergency and was desperate for cash. People keep cows for this reason. They're like a bank for local people, rising in value each year and we'd been meaning to open an account. Local Fula tribesmen look after the cow herds. They graze them in the bush. You don't pay for this service, but the herdsman makes his money by selling the milk. If our cow has a calf, that will be ours. Our plan is to bring it to our land in the rainy season when there are loads of weeds that it'll eat. Then we'll have a fertiliser source for the fruit trees.

We had also had a further nine additions to the family – the eggs from our hens hatched on my birthday. Donald and Daphne, our ducks, produced four ducklings, but sadly they didn't last too long. I found myself patching up a broken window in the poultry house to keep the snakes and Morris the monitor lizard out, but there are now new eggs and hopefully new life on the way.

There were by now five people calling me "Daddy". Gulliver obviously; Yama, a Gambian girl who helps cook and clean; Fakeba the gardener; Khady and Jumbo.

For Gulliver's first birthday, we bought him a drum. He loved to bang mine and head-bangs whenever he hears *djembe*. Apparently I also annoyed everyone as a toddler with my toy drum. On 31 March, I burnt a cake in our new mud-brick pizza oven and we invited the local kids around. There's no local tradition of celebrating birthdays here, but that doesn't mean we can't start one.

After working on the main house for several months it was nearly finished and the rains were yet to start. Everything was going to plan and I was happy. Bar a few unexpected expenses we'd had no major problems. As it was four times the size of our small house, I worked on the assumption that the roof would cost four times that one, but it seems it doesn't work that way. Not least because I have to include some huge beams of red wood as the combined weight of palm struts and straw is so *lebby lebby* (heavy).

Although I've had to tut, suck my cheeks in and huff and puff a little with some of the prices, the total is laughably small by Western standards. A short internet search revealed my main house, with a diameter of fourteen metres, to be cheaper than a luxury garden shed in the UK.

THINGS FALL APART

I am hurtling through a pitch-black forest. Headlamps pick out ultra-green ferns and the bright orange mud of the road. Occasionally a villager looms out of the darkness, causing me to swerve. Mile after mile there is pothole after pothole. Sometimes it feels as if the ground is giving way, the car plunging down and down until engine heaving, I lurch forwards, slither up the bank and down into another pit. I am starving, aching from the strain and covered in dirt.

Later, I'm sitting under the stars in my garden, the faint conical silhouette of my bespoke house before me. The chirrup of insects provides a midnight serenade and Khady is dishing up a plate of juicy, zingy mango plucked straight from our own tree. Heaven and hell in a heartbeat.

It had been a tough week. My car broke down, my solar batteries packed up, the people that sold us roof straw aggressively demanded more money, plus other assorted irritations. Then, we found out our motorbike had been trashed. I'm hoping things will turn around soon as I'm getting tired and don't know how much more I can take. In the evening, as I wearily sat down to rest I heard a hiss.

A loud hiss, like a dragon exhaling. I walked out and stood on what I thought was a stick. Obviously not. The bright-green snake whiplashed under my foot, which I'm not ashamed to say made me ... no, I'm ashamed to say.

The week started off okay. I drove to the Gambia in Kermit, intending to buy the electrical goods for the new house. Halfway there, I felt the clutch pedal weakening and the gears became hard to change. I ground to a halt. Kermit's generally been very reliable, but this clutch problem seemed to be never ending and it is all down to a rubber washer. No one seems to have an original and so it's always replaced with a Chinese part that lasts a few weeks at most. Every time I have a problem I'm told it's the rubber.

I had a spare and replaced it. After crossing the border I continued up to Banjul, but after 10 miles or so, the problem recurred. This time I called Amadou Landrover, my Gambian mechanic. He arrived in a jiffy on his bicycle and we went back to his workshop, a mango tree, where we finally fitted an original rubber. While we were at it, I told him that the brakes were feeling weak. The pads were fine so he checked under the hood and declared the problem. The rubber. The bloody, sodding rubber.

At four o'clock, later than planned and still not having managed to stop for breakfast or lunch, I continued up to the main commercial area and went to several Indian-run electrical shops. I'm installing a powerful solar system that will enable us to have a fridge, television and run my computer. I bought the solar panel, the battery and the rest of the paraphernalia.

By now I was hot and ravenous, so decided to head for a bite to eat in Brikama, a market town near the Senegalese border. As I approached, the sky turned black. It was a beautiful sight: pitch-black sky ahead and bright sunlight behind. The heavens opened and I crept forwards with wipers on full and the windows steaming up.

It's rare that I come across a traffic jam, but Brikama flooded in minutes and I sat for an hour without moving. The concept of queueing hasn't taken off in Africa and everyone drove ahead or on the verges, trying to inch forwards, thus grinding already slow traffic to a halt. It was getting dark and there wasn't time to eat or even to cross at the regular road border, where the roads are closed after dark. The only option was to take the smugglers' route through the forest. This at least reduced the risk of paying a bribe to bring my electrical goods into Senegal.

After a storm and especially at dusk, the sky is often stunning and this was no exception with a huge orange sky, silhouetted palm trees and big, white fluffy clouds in the background. Then it began. The road turned into a slithering mass of wet oozing red mud, darkness fell and for the next couple of hours I inched forward slowly, from pothole to pothole, some so large they practically consumed the vehicle.

At last I emerged onto the main road, relatively unscathed besides losing a license plate. Great, I can't wait to try to replace that. I meandered around small lumps of sleeping goat and larger lumps of sleeping cow. I was only a few miles from Abene when there was a horrible metallic grinding sound beneath me. The kind you really don't want to hear in a car. It was getting on for midnight. I decided to risk it and drive home but before I'd travelled a further mile there was a big bang, a puff of smoke and the engine seized. The car skidded to a stop in about half a second. I sat, shaken and whiplashed.

Midnight, pitch black on an African country road. At least it hadn't happened in the jungle. I searched for my phone but couldn't find it. (The next day I discovered it slid beneath the passenger seat.) I stumbled my way back to the nearest house in pitch blackness (the torch is on the phone) and a man there offered to take me home on his motorbike. An offer I accepted after we'd lugged all the solar equipment out of Kermit and into his house for safe keeping. We drove to my home cross-country along roads so slimy I stopped him after a mile or so. My pounding heart couldn't take it any more, sliding through mud on the back of the bike. I preferred to walk.

I eventually arrived to find a worried Khady, who immediately fed me underneath a big starry sky and brought hot water for a shower. Things were looking up. At 6.30am I left on my bicycle to check on Kermit whilst Khady tried to organise a mechanic. She had an appointment with the police that morning as they were deciding whether to imprison her cousin, our former motorcycle driver.

I waited for the mechanic all morning, sitting in Kermit and chatting to various passersby, slowly warming up as the car turned into an oven. I thought I could go to a local shop and order a coffee whilst I waited. But no. It was the first day of Ramadan, and so even that minor pleasure was denied.

After this experience, I thought, well at least I have my family and a lovely new house.

Then the house fell down.

I was enjoying a chat in the village with a friend, recounting all my woes. Fakeba, the lad working with us, drove past on our motorbike looking grim faced; I thought it odd that he didn't wave. I received a call from Khady.

"Can you come home quick?"

"Why?"

"If you don't come, you'll never know."

That's true, so off I went.

I walked up the driveway, saw the new house that I'm so proud of, and then realised something wasn't right. Several guys were working in the centre of the house but were entirely visible. A wall had fallen down under the weight of the roof that they were in the process of installing.

At that point, I couldn't bring myself to go and look

more closely. Khady was on the phone to her builder uncle. She smiled.

"No problem," she said. "It's not the main supporting wall, just an internal one. It'll all be fixed tomorrow."

I wasn't so sure and laid on my bed, quietly whimpering.

When I eventually went to inspect, it seemed that one of the supporting posts hadn't been strong enough. The broken pieces crumbled in my fingers. The guys had now supported the roof and it would be a quick job to rebuild the wall and put right with an extra supporting concrete post. So, it wasn't a catastrophe but it was annoying – yet more time and cement to do it properly. Khady said her uncle skimped on the cement to try and help me save money. I don't ask for much, but the one thing I look for in a house is that it won't fall down on top of me.

Then Khady and the others called me over to discuss the real reason for the collapse.

"This is Africa, things are very dark here," she opened with. Everyone nodded sagely. I interjected, saying yeah, but there wasn't enough cement or support; the wall collapsed under the pressure.

"Yes, but it's because of 'mystic Africa' that that happened," said Khady. Then the phone rang and it was her marabout.

"Has something happened to the house?" he asked.

Nobody had telephoned him or sent a message in any way; he was calling out of the blue. Khady explained what had happened and he said he'd come tomorrow to organise mystical protection. Everyone except me was relieved. In the meantime, we were asked to make millet porridge and invite a bunch of children around to eat it. The first thought that came to my mind was that if this marabout knew about the wall falling down, maybe he was behind it. But, of course, that thought was ridiculed by everyone.

Khady then proceeded to highlight to me how much jealousy there is in the village surrounding her. "We have a beautiful baby, a good car, a lovely house and land, you're still young and not a Grandpa. Many girls like you; you stay here all year round. It's clear someone is jealous and has cast a spell on us. Believe me."

Diannah, the builder agreed. Even though he's a qualified mason and everyone could see the crumbling concrete, he was adamant there were mystical forces at work. This is the response to pretty much everything here. If you're ill, everyone knows there is a scientific medical reason, but who caused that? Mystical forces, of course. If something is not understood, many Africans will strongly believe the simplest magical solution.

I know we don't understand everything about the world around us, but I can't blindly accept fairy tales when there's plenty of evidence of what's caused a problem. In the same way, I've seen Buddhists in Asia driving without regard to their own lives as it's karma and anyway they'll be reborn. No one has to take responsibility. The driver of the bus who crashed with me in it didn't need to worry about the fact that he was drunk. It was the will of Allah whether we'd crash.

I was proud, and perhaps a little smug, that we'd built a house that I'd designed. That smugness had come crashing down. It was as if when part of the structure fell down, my world crumbled with it. I suddenly felt very small, a stranger in a strange land. And an idiot. Although I'd come up with the design, I'd assumed the builders would ensure the correct procedures were followed to make it safe, and for the most part I'd been checking, but I'm no engineer. It's easy now to think how naïve I had been.

Despite the "no worries" attitude of the builders, I was seriously worried and so gladly accepted when a friend told me she knew a structural engineer in Ziguinchor and suggested he come and offer advice.

The engineer arrived, took one look and then showed me several problems. He left, telling me the entire roof needed to be removed. Not only that, but the whole building needed to be knocked down brick by brick, and then rebuilt. Oddly enough, that wasn't what I wanted to hear. Khady stormed off and wouldn't speak to me. I sat up all night, staring into space and swatting mosquitoes. I was ready to quit my dream. Then it started raining. Really pouring.

In the morning, Fakeba came to speak to me. Everyone wanted to know why I had brought in the structural engineer, when the builders had already given me a solution.

"Why do *toubabs* think so much and complicate everything?" he asked, inadvertently citing a major reason why Africa is so underdeveloped and mostly collapsing at the seams.

I walked around, picking up lumps of the collapsed concrete post and crumbled it in my hand. It was all sand.

"It was the will of Allah that the post collapsed; why didn't the rest of the house fall down?"

The builders said that the wall collapsing outwards was a good sign. Had it fallen inwards, that would have foreseen a death in the family. I started to laugh hysterically. The situation was very difficult for Khady, stuck between her family who were doing the building, loyalty to me, and her traditional beliefs.

The engineer returned and spent an hour or two in discussion with the builders, eventually reaching a mutual decision that they would put in extra support and finish the roof, thus saving the one thousand bales of straw I had sitting ready to be destroyed by rain and termites if it wasn't installed quickly. Then extra support posts could be built alongside the existing ones. The engineer was satisfied that if we did this, the house would be perfectly stable.

I was happy and relieved with this technical solution. Meanwhile Khady, under instructions from the marabout, had made porridge for the local children, who crowded around laughing and shouting. Before too much time passed, I was smiling again. It's going to take longer, but we will have the house of our dreams and we'll be able to sleep soundly knowing that it is safe and strong. And someday, the smaller house that we are still living in will become a guest house, adding to our income and perhaps turning into a real business. As Khady wisely pointed out, along with the good fortune that no one was hurt, it's far better that this happened now rather than later on. Besides, this is Africa. It is very dark and mysterious here, and people do skimp on cement.

This morning I picked my first mango from a tree I own and it is delicious. One of those special moments I will never forget. Khady's now grilling fish, Gulliver is happily playing with Bandit, our new puppy, and the sunset is one of those big orange ones from a holiday brochure.

This is Africa and today Africa hugs me.

EPILOGUE

A lot has happened since the events in this book which – aside from a few flashbacks – cover just over one year of my life in Senegal, from March 2012 to June 2013.

We did eventually finish the house, just before the rainy season truly began. I am slowly painting each room and decorating it with art from across the continent, an eclectic library and big, chunky bamboo furniture. We installed our own water system, water pumped out of our well into a tower that gravity-feeds the taps. Turning on the tap of my shower for the first time was a magic moment – three years is a long time to bucket shower.

The garden is my pride and joy and a photo from one year ago reveals that then we had a desert, whereas now we have a jungle. I can't wait to see how it'll look 10 years from now.

Khady always has a new business idea on the go. Earlier she was selling fish to remote villages and now she's opened a breakfast café in downtown Abene. She also continues to run her life via the advice of marabouts – which is great for gathering new stories to tell, but occasionally exhausting for this toubab. At the moment I'm showering twice a day in a liquid that smells like cow dung, in order to ensure that this book becomes a best seller. If it does, the marabout will have done his job. And if not, perhaps I should have showered three times a day.

Kermit the car continues to hop although the frequent roadblocks wear me down. I conducted a three-week tour of the surrounding area in early 2014 which was fantastic, but taught me an important lesson: I now employ an African driver for longer trips, which leaves me free to talk and guide our guests without the stress that being a toubab on the road brings with it.

We've received a steady stream of paying guests, mostly through my website, but also through personal recommendations. I'm having to refer people elsewhere for the busy Christmas period, as we've been fully booked for months. Twenty or more guests (some of whom camp) dancing to a *Koumpo* performance with half the village joining in is truly a scene to witness.

My guests have been, without exception, great people who are enthusiastic about African culture and art, or who are merely after a tranquil beach holiday. As much as I love my African family, it's important for me to "blah blah" in English now and again. The feedback has been gratifying, with blush-inducing raves posted on TripAdvisor. (You can read the reviews via a link on the front page of my website.) We're also receiving positive attention in guidebooks, with a notable mention in the new travel guide to Senegal published by Bradt.

Not long ago, I went to Dakar, ostensibly to sort out passports and a visa for Khady and Gulliver to come and see my home country, but there was also another task that I hoped to achieve. I walked along sand streets, searching for a beach bar that I'd frequented a couple of years earlier. Eventually I found the place and asked for Ibrahima, the *Baye Fall* who had given me my first gris-gris and started me on this long African adventure. One lad recognised the name, but told he had long gone.

In late 2014, as I finished this book, Khady and I saw another chameleon walking past the verandah of our home. As before she rushed over, pulled out a swollen breast and with the accuracy of a professional hit man, fired a stream of milk into the poor creature's face. The reason? We now have a new baby boy, Alfouseynou (Alfie) Fenton, named in honour of Khady's father. The squirting continues.

Simon Fenton, Senegal, 2015

Further Information

If you want to find out more about Simon's home, his guest house and see his pictures of the Little Baobab and Abene, please visit his website at: **www.thelittlebaobab.com**

Simon maintains a personal website highlighting his writing and photography, including a blog that he usually updates at least once a week at: **www.anaccidentalafrican.com**

Tony, the blind traveller, is rapidly completing his task of visiting every country in the world. For more information and to see his book, please visit: **www.tonythetraveller.com**

For more information about, or to support the work of eradicating FGM and helping the African-based human-rights organisation Tostan, please visit: **www.tostan.org**

"Abarakas"
(Acknowledgements)

After working for years as a farmer in Vietnam I read a book by a traveller to that beautiful country. I remarked to a friend that I'd had better experiences and I could have written a book. His reply was simple:

"But you didn't, did you?"

This time I wrote the book.

I dipped my toe into literary waters with a blog which seemed to me the perfect medium to publish anecdotes, diary entries, photos and so on. I thought that even if I didn't have a book in me, surely everyone needed to know the weird things I've eaten and how I was once spooked by an aardvark.

I was delighted and surprised to reach readers around the world, many of whom I've never actually met and I'd like to thank them for the great feedback which encouraged me to carry on writing.

Spanish author Javier Revertes and my cousin Paul led me to Eye Books where Dan, Martha and Jenny have worked wonders and toned down the "quirky Fenton-style things."

The magnificent cover was painted by Dutch artist and Abene resident, Bert Stiekma.

A big *abaraka* to my many friends in Senegal and all of our guests at the Little Baobab.

Without Khady it's hard to imagine life in Abene. She's my guide, teacher and best friend in this strange land.

Last but not least, thank you to my family in England who have always encouraged me to follow my heart. Mum, Dad, Jeremy, Karen, Edie: I'm sorry I followed it so far!

About Eye Books

Eye Books is a small independent publisher that passionately believes the more you put into life the more you get out of it.

It publishes stories that show ordinary people can and do achieve extraordinary things.

Its books celebrate "living" rather than existing.

It is committed to ethical publishing and tries to minimise its carbon footprint in the manufacturing and distribution of its books.

www.eye-books.com

eye books
About Extraordinary Things Done by Ordinary People

About the Author

Simon Fenton is a travel writer and photographer. After an early career in the morgues and pools of southern England, he lived, worked and travelled in Asia for several years, travelling independently through bush, mountain, desert and jungle, financing himself by teaching English, acting in Bollywood movies and working as a pig farmer in Vietnam.

He returned to "settle down", got married and set up the award-winning social enterprise StreetShine before a perfect storm of events re-ignited his wanderlust.

He found himself in Senegal, where he now lives with his Senegalese partner, Khady and their sons Gulliver and Alfie.

Simon built and runs his own guest house, information for which can be found at www.thelittlebaobab.com

You can keep up with Simon, his writing, photography and regular blog at www.anaccidentalafrican.com